Richard Lovett

Irish pictures

Richard Lovett

Irish pictures

ISBN/EAN: 9783744740197

Printed in Europe, USA, Canada, Australia, Japan

Cover: Foto ©Andreas Hilbeck / pixelio.de

More available books at **www.hansebooks.com**

IRISH PICTURES

Drawn with Pen and Pencil

BY

RICHARD LOVETT M.A.

AUTHOR OF 'NORWEGIAN PICTURES,' 'PICTURES FROM HOLLAND,' Etc.

WITH A MAP AND ONE HUNDRED AND THIRTY-THREE ILLUSTRATIONS FROM PHOTOGRAPHS AND SKETCHES.

ARDMORE, COUNTY WATERFORD.

NEW YORK
SCRIBNER & WELFORD

THE RELIGIOUS TRACT SOCIETY
56 PATERNOSTER ROW AND 164 PICCADILLY
1888

A CONNAUGHT CABIN.
(From a Sketch by Charles Whymper.)

CONTENTS AND LIST OF ILLUSTRATIONS.

CHAPTER I.

IRELAND'S EYE.

CHAPTER I.—*continued.*

CHAPTER II.

THE GARDEN OF IRELAND.

CHAPTER III.

THE VALLEY OF THE BOYNE.

CHAPTER IV.

FROM DUBLIN TO CORK.

CHAPTER V.

GLENGARIFF, KILLARNEY, AND VALENTIA.

CHAPTER V.—*continued.*

CHAPTER VI.

THE SHANNON.

CHAPTER VII.

CONNEMARA.

CHAPTER VIII.

THE DONEGAL HIGHLANDS.

CHAPTER IX.

BELFAST, ARMAGH, AND LONDONDERRY.

CHAPTER X.

THE GIANT'S CAUSEWAY, AND THE MOURNE MOUNTAINS.

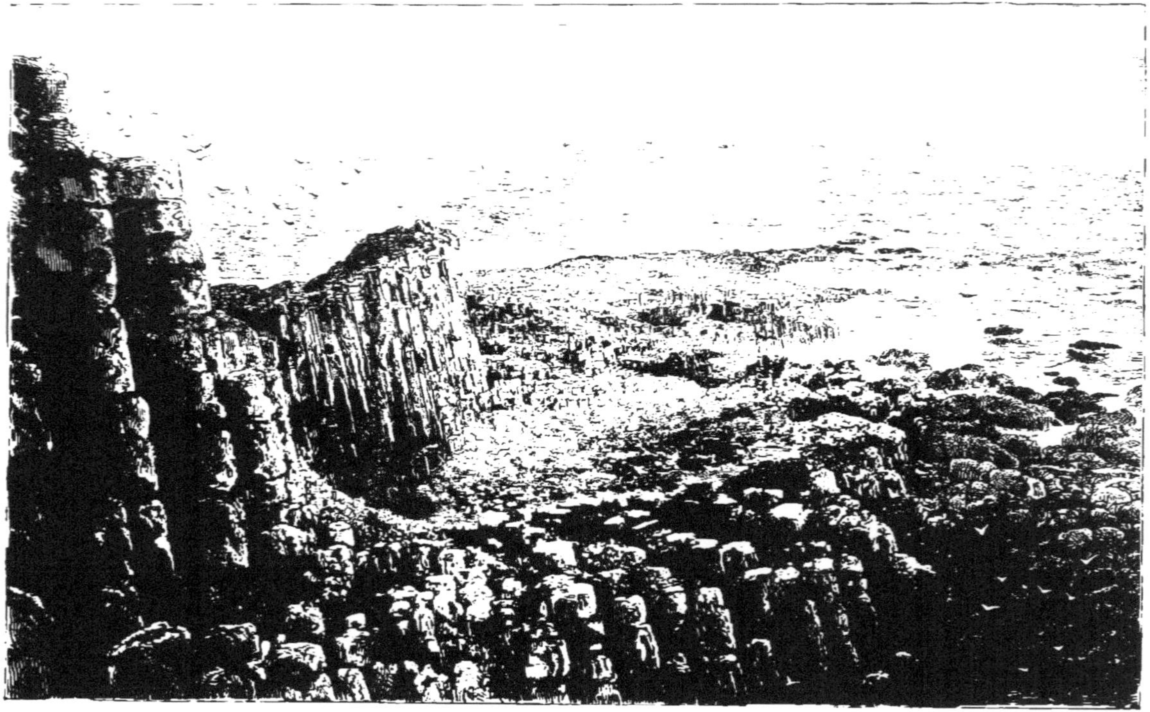

The Giant's Causeway.

HOLY CROSS ABBEY, TIPPERARY.

INTRODUCTION.

FOR some years past many of those acquainted with the 'Pen and Pencil Series' have expressed the wish that Ireland could be added to the list. *English Pictures* has long been a favourite; the more recent *Scottish Pictures* received a warm welcome; it seems hardly fair that the Emerald Isle should any longer be omitted.

It would be idle to deny that Ireland, even from this point of view, presents difficulties not experienced in the case of the sister kingdoms. Readers may naturally expect to find in any elaborate book upon Ireland issued at the present moment, some reference to the burning questions of

the hour; such, for example, as the relation of tenant to landlord, or the
expediency of Home Rule. Absorbing and important as these questions
are, the author trusts that it will not detract from either the interest or the
value of this work when the reader discovers they have been rigidly
excluded. It has not come within the author's province to discuss them.
His object is wider, and, it may be hoped, no less useful.

He seeks to give pen and pencil pictures of all parts of Ireland; to
produce upon the mind of the reader, so far as it is possible with the means
at his command, the impressions that a journey through the country would
make upon an observant and unprejudiced mind. This need not and does
not indicate indifference to political issues. Far from it. But evidence is
not lacking to show that the inhabitants of England, Scotland, and Wales do
not know as much as they might and ought about their Irish brethren, and
the land in which they dwell. The glorious scenery of Donegal and Kerry,
the picturesque ruins of Cashel and the Lower Shannon, the industries of
Belfast and Limerick, the splendid past of Ireland—her early Church-life,
her missionary enthusiasm, her literature, architecture, and art—present
many subjects for consideration and study that ought to command the
attention alike of ardent Nationalists, staunch Conservatives, and those who
may be unable to sympathise heartily with either section.

The United Kingdom possesses no fairer regions than Killarney and
Connemara; no wilder coast scenes than the lofty cliffs and bold headlands
that bear, at Valentia, Moher, Achill Island and Slieve League, the
whole unbroken force of the mighty Atlantic, and dash into driving foam its
wildest waves. There are no more interesting people among the rural
populations of Europe than such peasantry as the traveller meets in the
Golden Vale of Tipperary, along the mountain routes of Kerry, and amid
the lovely scenery of Galway, Donegal, Antrim, and Wexford.

Sad and troubled as much of the past of Ireland has been, she has no
reason to fear comparison in regard to the men she has produced. No
section of Great Britain can show abler men in their respective spheres of
life than Patrick[1] and Columba, Brian Boru and Shane O'Neill, James
Ussher and Bishop Berkeley, the Duke of Wellington and Lord Gough,
Oliver Goldsmith and Edmund Burke, Henry Grattan and Daniel O'Connell.

There is so much information, both interesting and also not generally
known, connected with the early Irish Church, with various periods of Irish
history, and with the art and architecture of Ireland, that the author had

---

[1] The Scotch claim Patrick as being born on their soil. This, though probable, is not certain; yet his
influence and work were certainly Irish.

contemplated giving separate chapters to each of these subjects. But
limitations of space, and the fact that these 'Pen and Pencil' volumes are
intended for popular reading, have compelled him in this respect to depart
from his original plan. But he has not felt it right to omit these important
subjects altogether, and hence they have been briefly treated as each seems to
arise naturally in the progress of the work. For example, the description of
the Royal Irish Academy Museum in Dublin has been made somewhat full,
in order that the chief peculiarities of Irish art, as illustrated by its most
brilliant achievements, may be indicated. The MSS. of Trinity College
Library have been referred to at length, to enable the reader to appreciate
the marvellous ability of the ancient scribes who wrote and illuminated them.
The personal history of St. Patrick naturally accompanies a description of
Slane and of Tara Hill, as some reference to that of St. Columba naturally
fits in with a description of Donegal. The origin and uses of the Round
Towers—that vexed question—cannot be passed over, and it is dealt with in
the description of Clonmacnois, where, within a few yards of each other, two
very fine examples have stood for centuries. In this less formal way he has
sought—he trusts not less satisfactorily—to deal with all these subjects.

The author has had to treat the religious difficulties of Ireland in much
the same way as the political. The tangled and tragic story of the past is
one that neither Protestant nor Roman Catholic can find any pleasure in
recalling. The conflicting currents and forces that influence the religious
life of Ireland to-day have been briefly indicated in the chapter on Belfast.
Notwithstanding the experience of the past, and the evidence of so much
that is conflicting in the present, the author ventures to hope that better
times are in store for the sister kingdom.

The writer has sought to give brief, pointed, and accurate descriptions
of all that is most distinctive in Irish scenery; to present a varied and
thoroughly representative series of engravings; to glance at some of the
most noteworthy men and deeds of the past; and to catch and depict, so
far as his pen can, the most typical aspects of the Ireland of to-day.

How far he has been successful must be decided by those who have
already given a kindly welcome to *Norwegian Pictures*, and *Pictures from
Holland*. He can only hope that the Irish readers into whose hands the
book may fall will accept his appreciation of, and admiration for, the land
they love so well as some atonement for the failings they may observe in
his work. As for other readers, he will feel amply rewarded for the time
and labour expended upon *Irish Pictures* if the book enlarges their know-

ledge of the land known more than fourteen centuries ago as 'the Sacred
Isle,' and helps to promote brotherly sympathy towards a people whose
history has for some centuries in varied phases been so closely interwoven
with that of the English, Welsh, and Scottish races.

The author would gratefully acknowledge the help so courteously given
to him by the large number of those whom he met during his various
journeys through Ireland, or to whom he applied for special information.
He had many opportunities of testing the courtesy and hospitality of the
Irish people, and, like others who have borne similar testimony, never found
these fail.

EDMUND BURKE.

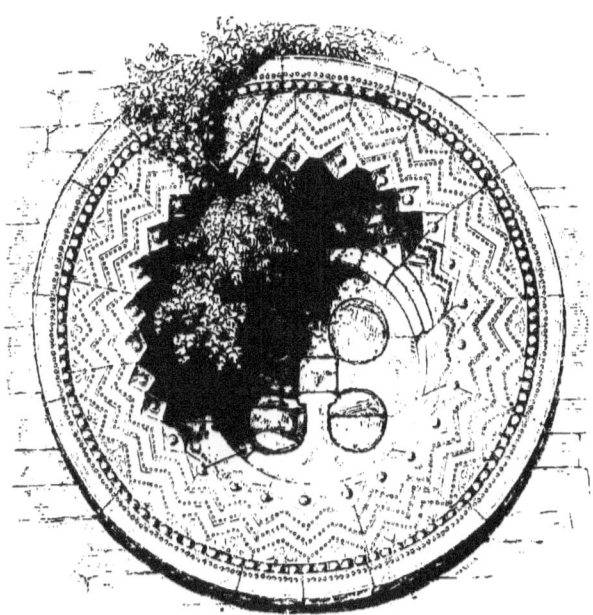

AN ANCIENT CIRCULAR WINDOW IN THE CHURCH AT RATHAIN, NEAR TULLAMORE.

A List of some of the most important Works consulted in the preparation of this Book.

The books included in this list are all important in their respective departments, and they are printed here as a convenient reference list for any who may wish to study somewhat more fully the various subjects of interest connected with Ireland and the Irish people. The list makes no pretension to completeness. It only seeks to indicate a selection of the most important and most easily accessible works.

ANNALS OF THE KINGDOM OF IRELAND.—By Four Masters. Translated by John O'Donovan. 4 vols. quarto. 1851.
ULSTER JOURNAL OF ARCHÆOLOGY, 1853–1861.—9 vols. small quarto.
THE JOURNALS OF THE ROYAL HISTORICAL AND ARCHÆOLOGICAL ASSOCIATION OF IRELAND.
DESCRIPTIVE CATALOGUE OF THE ROYAL IRISH ACADEMY.—By Sir W. Wilde.
HISTORY OF IRELAND.—By Keating.
IRISH NAMES OF PLACES.—By P. W. Joyce, LL.D. 2 vols. crown 8vo.

NATIONAL MSS. OF IRELAND.—By John T. Gilbert.

ADAMNAN'S LIFE OF ST. COLUMBA.—Edited by Dr. Reeves. 1 vol. quarto, 1857.

ST. PATRICK, APOSTLE OF IRELAND.—By Dr. Todd. 1 vol. octavo, 1864.

THE TRIPARTITE LIFE OF ST. PATRICK.—Edited for the Rolls Series by Dr. Whitley Stokes. 2 vols. octavo, 1887.

THE WRITINGS OF ST. PATRICK.—Revised translation by G. T. Stokes, D.D., and C. H. H. Wright, D.D. 1 vol. octavo, paper cover, 1888.

IRELAND AND THE CELTIC CHURCH.—By G. T. Stokes. 1 vol. crown 8vo.

THE ROUND TOWERS AND ANCIENT CHRISTIAN ARCHITECTURE OF IRELAND.—By Dr. Petrie. 1 vol. quarto, 1845.

NOTES ON IRISH ARCHITECTURE.—By the late Earl of Dunraven. Edited by Miss Stokes. 2 vols. folio, 1875-1877.

EARLY CHRISTIAN ARCHITECTURE IN IRELAND.—By Miss Stokes.

EARLY CHRISTIAN ART IN IRELAND.—By Miss Stokes.

ECCLESIASTICAL HISTORY OF IRELAND.—By Dr. Killen. 2 vols. octavo.

THE DUBLIN PENNY JOURNAL, 1832-1836.—4 vols. royal octavo.

THE IRISH PENNY JOURNAL, 1841.—1 vol. royal octavo.

THE BOYNE AND THE BLACKWATER.—By Sir William Wilde. 2nd edition, 1850.

LOUGH CORRIB.—By Sir William Wilde.

THE DONEGAL HIGHLANDS.

TRAITS AND STORIES OF THE IRISH PEASANTRY.—By William Carleton. 2 vols. 8vo. 1867.

TALES AND STORIES OF THE IRISH PEASANTRY.—By William Carleton. 1 vol. 8vo. 1846.

FAIRY LEGENDS AND TRADITIONS.—By T. C. Croker.

THE BALLADS OF IRELAND.—Edited by E. Hayes. 2 vols. crown octavo. Boston, 1856.

DERRY AND ENNISKILLEN.—By Professor Witherow, D.D.

THE BOYNE AND AGHRIM.—By Professor Witherow, D.D.

IRELAND : ITS SCENERY, CHARACTER, ETC.—By Mr. and Mrs. S. C. Hall. 3 vols. octavo.

SKETCHES OF IRISH LIFE.—By Mrs. S. C. Hall. 1 vol. octavo.

MEMORIES OF A MONTH AMONG THE 'MERE IRISH.'—By W. H. Floredice. 1 vol. crown 8vo.

THE RELIGIOUS HISTORY OF IRELAND.—By James Godkin. 1 vol. 8vo. 1873.

AN ANCIENT IRISH BELL.

c

Trinity College and the Bank of Ireland, Dublin.

HOWTH HARBOUR AND IRELAND'S EYE.

CHAPTER I.

IRELAND'S EYE.

IRELAND'S EYE is the name of a rocky islet standing over against Howth Harbour, for many years the port of Dublin and the chief approach by sea to that capital. Kingstown and North Wall have superseded Howth Harbour; the rocky islet is now seen to advantage only by those who explore Howth itself; nevertheless the island's name is no bad description of Dublin. The great city is in more senses than one Ireland's Eye. Through it the Emerald Isle receives many of her impressions of the outer world, and no fairer feature in her wealth of natural beauty does she possess than the noble bay of Dublin, with the great city nestling beneath the bold headlands of Killiney and the Hill of Howth.

The first impression made upon the mind of the observer by Dublin is one of disappointment. The city hardly seems to live up to its environment. The scenery of the bay is very lovely, whether seen in the early morning or the late evening of a summer's day; the view up the Liffey as the

steamer approaches the North Wall, embracing the river, the crowded masts
and boats, the fine dome of the Custom House in the near foreground, and
the multitudinous roofs and spires of the city in the distance, is enticing, and
whets the appetite and expectations of the explorer. But here as elsewhere
the close inspection does not, at any rate at first, realize the distant promise.
It is not easy to define exactly the effect produced as one makes the
acquaintance of the quays, Sackville Street, St. Patrick's Cathedral, Merrion
Square, and College Green.   There are handsome buildings, wide streets,
spacious squares, many evidences of life, prosperity and abundance, and yet
something seems lacking. Dublin is not like London, New York, Paris, or
Amsterdam.   In these great cities, differing widely as they do in manifold
respects from each other, the evidences of prosperity predominate; in Dublin,
although she shares many of the best qualities of her larger sisters, the
stranger, although he may have a firm conviction that better times are
coming, hesitates to assert that she is manifestly prospering.

While this impression is strong, the visitor can readily imagine that
many take an early and sometimes incurable dislike to Dublin. The signs
of apparent poverty are plentiful; the streets and buildings that really please
the eye are few, the number of ragged children seems abnormal; and if
the visitor to St. Patrick's or Christ Church devotes any attention to the
neighbourhoods of these noted buildings, he meets many interesting but not
altogether pleasing pictures of human life. Yet the writer gladly admits that
Dublin's power to impress him favourably increased with each successive visit.
As he came to know her better, he grew to like her more, and to appreciate
more fully the beauty of her surroundings, and the special objects for which
she claims recognition.   And it is now time to turn to some of these.

Dublin is in the first place a considerable port. The Liffey, the quays,
the docks and the canals are among the most prominent features of the
metropolis. It is from the river, indeed, that she gets her name as well as
a large portion of her wealth. The ancient high road from Tara to Wicklow
crossed the river at this point in very early days by means of a rough wicker
or hurdle bridge. Naturally a city grew up around the bridge or ford, and
the name for Dublin in the Irish Annals is Ath-Cliath (pronounced Ah-clee),
'the ford of the hurdles.' Duibh-linn, 'the black pool' or 'river,' the ancient
name of this part of the Liffey, gradually banished the older, and has long
been the only name by which the city is known. The ancient ford is now
represented by splendid bridges, the cluster of huts has expanded into square
miles of brick and mortar, and the water which ages since floated the
coracles of the Irish or the warships of the Northmen is now ploughed by
the bulky steel ships of modern commerce. All else has changed marvellously, but in the very name of Ireland's capital there survives the sure
evidence of her former humility.

Many facilities both natural and artificial exist for giving those wishful to get them good representative views of Dublin. A favourite point of view is the top of the Nelson Monument, which towers aloft in the centre of Sackville Street. Seen thence the whole city lies spread out at the observer's feet, and from that elevation, as from no other, he can also observe the beauty of the surrounding country. Some very fine distant views are obtained at different parts of the Phœnix Park. But the true citizen of Dublin maintains that the view obtained from the O'Connell Bridge is not only the best that the city can show, but is also equal to the best that any rival capital possesses. On the left bank of the Liffey, a short distance below the great bridge, stands one of the most prominent buildings in the city, viz. the Custom House.

THE CUSTOM HOUSE, DUBLIN.

Dublin is not only the eye but the heart of Ireland. Hence on every side are traces of the many-sided life of the nation. Her antiquity is evident in many of her names. Her former national life is recalled by the building that is now the Bank of Ireland. It was here in former days the Irish Parliament met, and here many of Curran's and Grattan's famous speeches were delivered. Her relation to England is kept prominently in view by the towers and courtyard of Dublin Castle. Her educational and literary life of the last three centuries has largely centred in Trinity College, which fronts boldly and closely upon an open space in the very heart of the city, the famous College Green. To her great religious hero is dedicated one of her two ancient cathedrals, and though the statement that St. Patrick founded it is mere fancy, it is fitting that he should for centuries have been thus associated with the metropolitan life. In the centre of College Green, and facing the fine façade of Trinity College, stands the statue of Grattan, while before the gateway of the great university, fronting the effigy of Ireland's renowned orator, are placed statues of Edmund Burke and Oliver Goldsmith. Brilliant political oratory, fervid patriotism, noble eloquence, far-seeing statesmanship, and undying literary fame are here concentred and kept continually before the eyes and the minds of the multitudes who daily throng Grafton Street and College Green.

And indeed here is the true heart of Dublin. Much of the business of the city is carried on in this district ; much of her intellectual activity here finds its home and field of work ; the financial heart of the country throbs here, and here blend the associations of the present and the memories of the past in stronger and more vigorous union than elsewhere.

The foundation of Trinity College dates from 1592, and the institution began the work of teaching in 1593 as 'the College of the Holy and Indivisible Trinity near Dublin,' in the buildings of the Augustinian monastery of All Hallows. During the reigns of James I. and Charles I. it was richly endowed with confiscated lands. Many private benefactors enriched it. James I. conferred also the privilege it still enjoys of sending two members to Parliament. It was not until 1792 that a Roman Catholic could there take a degree, and not until 1873 could any member of that communion enjoy any part of the rich endowments possessed by the College.

The façade facing College Green is somewhat heavy and sombre. It is very massive, and is principally built of Portland stone ; but it at once arrests the attention of the passer-by, and the effect is by no means unpleasing. Passing between the statues of Burke and Goldsmith which flank the entrance, the visitor is admitted into a spacious quadrangle, in the centre of which stands a tall, handsome bell-tower, built of granite. On his right hand stands the Examination Hall or Theatre, and on the left the Chapel, with the Dining Hall as its next neighbour. Both Halls are enriched with portraits of famous students and graduates.

But it is to the right of the bell tower that most visitors make their first pilgrimage, for there stands the handsome range of buildings containing the Library. It is included among the five great libraries of the kingdom entitled to a copy of every book published in Great Britain and Ireland. The structure, from an architectural point of view, is plain and unpretending, and yet, withal, possesses a dignity of its own, and a certain fitness as the home of a great literary collection. The ground floor consists chiefly of an arcade, and the library building occupies the rest of the structure. The main apartment is the splendid gallery containing the bulk of the books. This is 210 feet long, 41 feet wide, and 40 feet high. The wood is dark, old oak, and along each side are recesses placed at right angles to the main axis of the room, filled with shelves, and arranged so as to combine

very happily architectural effect with economy of space. A gallery, placed
about twenty feet above the level of the floor, runs round the room, and
the best view of this magnificent chamber can be obtained from the end
of this gallery immediately over the entrance. The visitor, if at all literary
in his sympathies, cannot fail to be charmed as his eye travels down the

TRINITY COLLEGE LIBRARY, INTERIOR.

whole length of the room. The long vista, the lights streaming across from
the windows at the end of each recess, the lofty arched roof, the apparently
numberless bookshelves and books, the comfortable tables below with their
busy readers, the cases full of priceless MSS., the long rows of gleaming
marble busts of distinguished literary men of all ages and lands, the time-

worn volumes and the richly carved and deep-toned wood, both alike
eloquent of age—all these combine not only to delight the eye, but also at
once to stimulate and to satisfy one's sense of literary fitness. A feeling of
content that such a splendid library should be so superbly housed steals over
the observer.

There are many matters in Ireland wherein ordinary courses of pro-
cedure seem to be reversed. The origin of Trinity College Library is an
illustration in point. In various countries and in all ages scholars and lovers
of literature have had to bewail the ravages in the way of MS. and book

destruction caused by war. Yet it is out of warfare that this great library appears to have sprung.
In 1603 the Spaniards were defeated at the battle
of Kinsale by the English and Irish. The victors
in their enthusiasm resolved to erect some permanent monument of their success ; they collected
among themselves the sum of £1,800 and—would
that their example had found many imitators !--
decided to expend the money in the purchase of
books, and present them as the nucleus of a
library to the College at Dublin, then completing
its first decade. Archbishop Usher was appointed
to expend the money, and few
of the many tasks he performed
during his life can have been so
congenial. Since his day the
collection has grown and grown
until now it ranks as one of the
largest in Europe. It can claim
the Bodleian as a twin brother,
for while Usher was spending
his soldiers' money in London,
he met there Sir T. Bodley, who
was purchasing books for his
Oxford collection.

INITIAL, THE LETTER L, FROM THE BOOK OF KELLS.

Usher's own library, one which embraced manifold treasures in its
10,000 volumes, found here a permanent home. At the eastern end of the
library is a handsome room, 52 feet long, 26 wide, and 22 high, containing
what is known as the Fagel Library, once the property of a gentleman
named Fagel, Pensionary of Holland, comprising 17,000 volumes, and
purchased for £8,000.

The library is very rich in specimens of early Irish illuminated MSS.,
and these, together with many other very precious literary treasures, have
their home in what is called the Manuscript Room. This apartment is on

the ground floor, and can only be seen by visitors who are able to secure the presence of the Librarian or one of the Fellows of the College.

The most famous of these literary treasures are exhibited in cases which stand on the floor of the great library, and among these the highest place is held by the Book of Kells. This is one of the finest MSS. in Europe, and as a specimen of Irish illumination and writing has no rival. It dates from the time when Ireland, under the name of Scotia, was famous throughout Europe for her schools and for her missionary enterprise. It was the product of the age which sent Columba to Iona, Cuthbert to England, and Columbanus to Gaul. It is a copy of the Gospels, and takes its name from the fact that it once belonged to the monastery at Kells in Meath. The date has to be fixed by internal evidence, and the best authorities now lean to the view that it was written about the end of the sixth century. The Irish Annals record that in the year 1006 it was stolen from the church at Kells, that it was famous for its cover, and that it was found after forty nights and two months,

PART OF AN ILLUMINATED MONOGRAM, FROM THE BOOK OF KELLS.

'after its gold had been taken from it, and with sods over it.' The monastery of Kells became Crown property in 1539, and the great MS. fell into the hands of Gerald Plunket of Dublin. In the seventeenth century Usher became its owner, and with his other books, in 1661, it found a permanent and safe home where it has since dwelt. To it, as to so many of its brethren, time and the binder have proved cruel foes. Although it still contains 344 folios, it has lost leaves at both the beginning and end; and when, in the early part of this century, it was rebound, the margins were sadly mutilated. But time has done little to destroy the wondrous beauty of colouring in its marvellous illuminations, and its wealth and richness of design are still the wonder of every competent observer. It is the most superb example of this branch of early Irish art. Professor Westwood thus describes the special features of this book as illustrative of the early Irish style of MS. adornment :

'Ireland may be justly proud of the Book of Kells—a volume traditionally asserted to have belonged to St. Columba, and unquestionably the most elaborately executed MS. of so early a date now in existence, far excelling in the gigantic size of the letters at the commencement of each Gospel, the excessive minuteness of the ornamental details crowded into whole pages, the number of its very peculiar decorations, the fineness of the writing, and the endless variety of its initial capital letters, the famous Gospels of Lindisfarne in the Cottonian Library. But this manuscript is still more valuable on account of the various pictorial representations of different scenes in the life of our Saviour, delineated in the genuine Irish style, of which several of the manuscripts of St. Gall and a very few others offer analogous examples. The numerous illustrations of this volume render it a complete storehouse of artistic interest. The text itself is far more extensively decorated than in any other now existing copy of the Gospels.'[1]

'Especially deserving of notice,' continues Professor Westwood, 'is the extreme delicacy and wonderful precision united with an extraordinary minuteness of detail with which many of these ancient manuscripts were ornamented. I have examined with a magnifying-glass the pages of the Gospels of Lindisfarne and Book of Kells, for hours together, without ever detecting a false line or an irregular interlacement ; and when it is considered that many of these details consist of spiral lines, and are so minute as to be impossible to have been executed without a pair of compasses, it really seems a problem not only with what eyes, but also with what instruments they could have been executed. One instance of the minuteness of these details will suffice to give an idea of this peculiarity. I have counted in a small space, measuring scarcely three quarters of an inch, by less than half an inch in width, in the Book of Armagh, not fewer than one hundred and fifty-eight interlacements of a slender ribbon pattern, formed of white lines edged by black ones upon a black ground.'[2]

'The introduction of natural foliage in this MS. is another of its great peculiarities, whilst the intricate intertwinings of the branches is eminently characteristic of the Celtic spirit, which compelled even the human figure to submit to the most impossible contortions.'[3]

The following inscription, in a minute hand, is still partly legible in a small semicircular space at the head of the columns on folio 4 verso.

'This work doth pass all mens conying that doth live in any place.

[1] *National MSS. of Ireland*, by John T. Gilbert, p. 14.   [2] *Ibid.* p. 20.   [3] *Ibid.* p. 15.

'I doubt not there. . . anything but that the writer hath obtained God's grace, GP.' On the verso of folio 344 is the following entry :—' I, Geralde Plunket, of Dublin, wrot the contents of every chapter ; I mean where every chapter doth begin, 1568. The boke contaynes tow hundreth v and iii leaves at this present xxvii August 1568.'

Under this is written by Usher, who was Bishop of Meath from 1621 to 1624 : 'August 24, 1621. I reckoned the leaves of this and found them to be in number 344. He who reckoned before me counted six score to the hundred.'[1]

While upon the subject of Irish illuminated MSS., and as they form such characteristic specimens of Irish art, we must refer to three others that enrich Trinity College Library. The first, the Book of Durrow, is a copy of the Gospels according to the Vulgate version. It gets its name from a monastery founded about 523 A.D. by Columba, at Durrow, or *Dairmag*, the Plain of Oaks, in King's County. Tradition has maintained that Columba wrote the MS., but the fact that the text of the MS. does not appear to be the same as that in use in Ireland in the sixth century tells against this view. On the back of folio 12 is an entry in Latin to this effect : ' I pray thy blessedness, O holy presbyter, Patrick, that whosoever shall take this book into his hands may remember the writer, Columba, who have myself written this Gospel in the space of twelve days by the grace of our Lord.'

Like several other of these ancient MSS., this copy of the Gospels once possessed a silver *cumdach* or shrine. This has unfortunately perished, but the inscription upon it has been preserved. It ran ' The prayer and benediction of St. Columb Kille be upon Flann, the son of Malachi, King of Ireland, who caused this cover to be made.'

Flann reigned 879–916 A.D., and at that early date the book had become an object of special veneration. In the Annals of Clonmacnois, the translator, Connell Mageoghegan refers to a superstitious belief once current with regard to this and other early books. ' He (Columba) wrote three hundred books with his own hand. They were all New Testaments ; he left a book to each of his churches in the kingdom, which books have a strange property, which is, that if they or any of them had sunk to the bottom of the deepest waters, they would not lose one letter, or sign, or character of them ; which I have seen tried, partly by myself on that book of them which is at Dorowe (Durrow) in the King's Co., for I saw the ignorant man that had the same in his custody, when sickness came on cattle, for their remedy, put water on the book and suffer it to rest therein ; and saw also cattle return thereby to their former state ; and the book receive no loss.'

The water-stained condition of some of the last leaves of the Book of Durrow confirms the accuracy of the scribe's statement as to the experiments to which ages ago it was subjected.

[1] *National MSS. of Ireland,* pp. 20, 21.

We are able to give a very fine specimen of one of the illuminated pages of this MS.

The second example, the Book of Dimna, so called after the name of the scribe who wrote it, a copy of the Gospels in Latin, dates most probably from the seventh century. It once belonged to the abbey of Roscrea. It was encased in a shrine about the middle of the tenth century. 'The shrine with its precious enclosure disappeared at the time of the dissolution of monasteries; it was found by boys hunting rabbits in the year 1789, among the rocks of the Devil's Bit Mountain in the county of Tipperary, carefully preserved and concealed. The boys who discovered it tore off the silver plate and picked out some of the lapis-lazuli with which it was studded. It then came into the possession of Dr. Harrison of Nenagh, and after passing through the hands of Mr. Monck Mason, Sir William Betham, and Dr. Todd, was finally purchased for the library.'[1]

AN ILLUMINATED PAGE FROM THE BOOK OF DURROW.

The third and in some respects the most interesting of all is the Book of Armagh, a curious composite volume of very great importance in the literary history of Ireland, and in regard to the life of St. Patrick. Dr. Reeves has discovered evidence in the MS. itself that renders it almost certain that it was written about A.D. 807 by a scribe named Ferdomnach. It seems to have been referred to by the Annalists as 'the Canon of Patrick,' and they record that in 937 it

[1] Miss Stokes' *Early Christian Art in Ireland*, p. 24.

was enclosed in a case by Donogh, the son of Flann, King of Ireland. At a later stage the ancient silver case was enclosed in a leather cover, and of this we are able to give an illustration. It presents a typical example of Irish ornamentation. An entry at the foot of folio 16 purports to have been made in the presence of the far-famed Brian Boru. In that case it was most probably done in 1002, when that king offered twenty ounces of gold on the altar of Armagh. In ancient days, according to the usual custom, the book had a *maor* or keeper, who received an endowment of land in virtue of his office. His descendants were known as *Mac maor*, 'sons of the keeper,' and in time this became Mac Moyre. Upon the reverse of one leaf appears, under the date of 1662, the signature of Florentinus Moyre, the last of the family who held the guardianship of the book. This man went in 1680 to London to give evidence in a trial, and, before starting, placed the book in pledge for five pounds. Soon after, the MS. and its leather case came into the hands of Arthur Brownlow; it remained in the Brownlow family

LEATHER OUTER CASE OF THE BOOK OF ARMAGH, SHOWING THE EARLY IRISH TRACERY ORNAMENTATION.

until 1853, when Dr. Reeves purchased it, and handed it over to the late Primate Beresford, who in his turn presented it to the Library.

'The Book of Armagh is now defective at the commencement. Its first surviving portion is occupied with notes in Latin and Irish on St. Patrick's acts, a collection styled *Liber Angueli*, relating to the rights and prerogatives of the See of Armagh, and the Confession of St. Patrick. These are followed by St. Jerome's letter to Damasus, Eusebian Canons, and preface to the New Testament; interpretation of Hebrew names; Gospels of Matthew,

Mark, Luke, John; Epistles of Paul, including that to the Laodiceans, with prefaces, chiefly by Pelagius; Acts of Apostles; and Life of St. Martin of Tours by Sulpicius Severus. Some of the pages are much rubbed, as if frequently exposed or touched, probably for the purpose of swearing.'

There are very interesting specimens to be seen here of other classes of MSS. Standing highest in general interest are those belonging to the Greek Testament. The Library possesses a valuable palimpsest, known as the *Codex Rescriptus Dublinensis;* it has been carefully edited by the present librarian, the Rev. T. K. Abbott. It is a small quarto volume, $8\frac{1}{2}$ inches by 6, consisting of 110 folios. It contains considerable portions of St. Matthew's Gospel, and its readings possess a very high critical value. It dates in all probability from the fifth century, and is known in the lists of authorities by the letter Z. Any one who wishes to appreciate Dr. Abbott's labours, and the enormous difficulty of much of the work done on behalf of recent New Testament scholarship by such men as Tischendorf and Tregelles, should inspect this MS. They will find it extremely difficult even to see, to say nothing of deciphering, the dim Greek uncial letters that were nearly obliterated many centuries ago, to make way for the later and less valuable writing placed over it.

The Library also possesses a much later MS. that has been rendered famous by a fortuitous event in Greek Testament controversy. It is well known that Erasmus omitted from the first edition of his Greek Testament the words in 1 John v. 7, 8, translated in our A.V., 'In heaven, the Father, the Word, and the Holy Ghost: and these three are one. And there are three that bear witness in earth.' When attacked for so doing, he promised that if a single Greek MS. could be found containing the words he would then insert them. They were at last found in a Greek MS., written in the cursive or running hand, of late date and very doubtful authority. This MS., known as the *Codex Monfortianus,* is also carefully kept in the Manuscript Room. Erasmus, true to his promise, although he did not believe the words to be genuine, inserted them in his third edition. The Revised Version omits them, as resting upon altogether insufficient authority.

But it is high time we left the Library for a stroll through the College itself.

The various departments of learning are all adequately housed within its very extensive precincts; the medical school being especially fortunate in this respect. The chemical lecture room and laboratory are splendidly equipped with all the latest and best facilities both for lecturing and practical work. The college park is also a very pleasant place of resort, and on the occasion of a University Cricket Match or Athletic Sports is thronged with the fashion and beauty of Dublin.

Across the street, and opposite to the north-west corner of Trinity

¹ *National MSS. of Ireland,* p. 23.

College, stands the considerable pile of building in which centres the work of the Bank of Ireland. Formerly the Irish Houses of Parliament met here. Visitors are still shown the room in which the Irish House of Lords met, and which, one is told, remains very much now as it appeared in the days of Castlereagh.

Dublin possesses two cathedrals, both of which, in recent years, have been thoroughly renovated and restored by private munificence. The younger, but in many respects the more interesting, is St. Patrick's. The early history of this building seems to be somewhat obscure. About 1190, Archbishop John de Comyn, the first English Archbishop of Dublin, built a collegiate establishment here on the site of a much older parish church, and in 1213 his successor changed the church into a cathedral. In 1362 it was burnt, and in 1370 it was rebuilt, with the addition of a fine tower. In 1542 its constitution was changed to that of a dean and chapter, and in 1546 it passed to the Crown. During this period it was neglected and fell into decay, but in 1554 Queen Mary restored its rights and privileges. It suffered during the Commonwealth troubles, and also at the hands of James II.'s soldiers in 1688. In 1713 the most famous man who has ever been associated with it, Jonathan Swift, was appointed to the deanery. From that time

THE CHOIR, ST. PATRICK'S CATHEDRAL.

until his death, in 1745, he devoted himself to the preservation of the building and its numerous monuments, and to the increase of its revenues. In 1783, the Order of St. Patrick was instituted, and the banners of the knights now hang in the choir. In 1865 the restoration effected by the wealth of the late Sir Benjamin Lee Guinness was completed. It had fallen into what seemed like hopeless decay, and although some partial attempts had been made to stay the progress of destruction, the building seemed doomed. But by the aid of Sir B. Guinness the building has been so restored that Sir James Ware's description once more applies: 'If we consider the compass, or the beauty, or the magnificence of its structure, in my opinion it is to be preferred before all the cathedrals in Ireland.'

The architecture of the structure is the First Pointed or Early English, and the ground-plan consists of a nave, choir, north and south transepts, all with aisles, and a Lady Chapel. The tower was built in 1370, and the granite spire, a prominent but not at all lovely object, was added to the tower in 1740. The building is 300 feet long, the nave 67 feet wide, the transepts 157 feet long and 80 feet wide, and the tower and steeple 221 feet high. Sir B. Guinness entirely rebuilt the north and south aisles.

JONATHAN SWIFT.

The interior is crowded with monuments, some few of them possessing very special interest. Chief among these is the one dedicated to Swift, who was buried October 22nd, 1745. It stands in the south aisle, and consists of a fine bust, and a slab upon which is inscribed the epitaph written by himself; one of the saddest inscriptions in this or any other cathedral. It is in Latin, but may be freely rendered: 'Here lies the body of Jonathan Swift, D.D., Dean of this cathedral church, where fierce indignation can no longer rend the heart. Go, traveller, and imitate, if thou canst, one who, as far as in him lay, was an earnest champion of liberty.' Close by is the inscription commemorating Mrs. Hester Johnson, or 'Stella,' as 'a person of extraordinary endowments and accomplishments, in body, mind and behaviour; justly admired and respected by all who knew her, on account of her many eminent virtues, as well as for her great natural and acquired perfections.' She was buried by the second pillar from the west door on the south side of the nave, Jan. 30th, 1728, seventeen years before the brilliant but bitter genius of Swift sank to rest.

Swift's life is a tragedy, perhaps the most tragical in the long story of English literature. One cannot look upon the two monuments without wishing that the fate of each might have been different, that Swift could have used his splendid intellect for the good rather than the injury of others, and that Stella's loving heart could have been fixed upon one in whose full and unselfish response she would have experienced a happier lot.

Thackeray's judgment to some seems harsh, but many facts bear it out.
'The *sæva indignatio*, of which he spoke as lacerating his heart, and which
he dares to inscribe on his tombstone—as if the wretch who lay under that
stone waiting God's judgment had a right to be angry—breaks out from
him in a thousand pages of his writing, and tears and rends him. Against
men in office, he having been overthrown; against men in England, he
having lost his chance of preferment there, the furious exile never fails to
rage and curse. In a note in his biography, Scott says that his friend
Dr. Tuke, of Dublin, has a lock of Stella's hair, enclosed in a paper by Swift,
on which are written, in the dean's hand, the words: "Only a woman's
hair." An instance, says Scott, of the dean's desire to veil his feelings
under the mask of cynical indifference. See the various notions of critics!
Do those words indicate indifference, or an attempt to hide feeling? Did
you ever hear or read four words more pathetic? Only a woman's hair:
only love, only fidelity, only purity, innocence, beauty, only the tenderest
heart in all the world stricken and wounded, and passed away now out of
reach of pangs of hope deferred, love insulted, and pitiless desertion:—only
that lock of hair left; and memory and remorse for the guilty, lonely
wretch, shuddering over the grave of his victim. And yet to have had so
much love, he must have given some. Treasures of wit and wisdom, and
tenderness too, must that man have had locked up in the caverns of his
gloomy heart, and shown fitfully to one or two whom he took there. But it
was not good to visit that place. People did not remain there long, and
suffered for having been there.'[1]

In the north transept stands a characteristic specimen of Swift's biting
satire, exercised, it must be admitted, more justly in this case than in many.
The Duke of Schomberg was killed at the Battle of the Boyne, and buried
in St. Patrick's. His relatives do not seem to have cared sufficiently for
the duke to contribute towards the cost of a monument in commemoration
of his qualities. The inscription, therefore, runs to the effect that the
Dean and Chapter had repeatedly and earnestly besought the duke's
relatives to erect the monument, that after letters, the requests of friends,
repeated and earnest entreaties had availed nothing, the Dean and Chapter
had at length erected the stone, in order that the visitor might know where
the ashes of Schomberg reposed. The sting is at the end, where it is
asserted that the duke's reputation for valour availed more with strangers
than his ties of blood did with his own kindred.

This is not flattering to the relatives of the duke, nor, on the other
hand, does their conduct indicate that they felt very deeply the loss of
the noted soldier; but it is hardly in accordance with fact to characterize
the inscription, as Macaulay does, by the phrase, 'a furious libel.'

An hour may be pleasantly spent in deciphering the various monuments

[1] Thackeray, *English Humourists.*

D

and inscriptions; but there are not many of general interest. In the south choir aisle is one in remembrance of the Rev. Charles Wolfe, author of the *Burial of Sir John Moore;* and in the churchyard one to the memory of Dr. Todd, the archæologist and author.

Only a few hundred yards separate St. Patrick's from the sister cathedral Christ Church. It is supposed to stand upon the site of the old Celtic *dun* or fort. It was founded in 1038, and completed in the following century by Richard Strongbow and others in conjunction with the Archbishop of Dublin, Laurence O'Toole. In 1562 the greater part of the structure fell in; and by subsequent restorations and vicissitudes most of the original building has disappeared. There is some reason to believe that originally it was a finer structure than St. Patrick's. Like its sister, it owes its present complete and beautiful appearance to the liberality of a Dublin brewer, Mr. Roe, who expended about a quarter of a million sterling upon it. The peculiar plan of the original choir was ascertained by examination of the crypts, and closely followed in the restoration. A short apsidal choir or presbytery stands to the east of the central tower, and around this an aisle or processional path runs, and beyond this to the east are two chapels, the smaller adjoining the choir. A Synod House for the meetings of the disestablished Episcopal Church of Ireland was erected and connected by a passage with the west end of the cathedral, the tower was raised, and the whole edifice practically rebuilt. It belongs to the transitional style of architecture. A few years ago Mr. Drew, architect to Christ Church, discovered the remains of the Chapter House, near which were formerly the old Law Courts of Dublin, and the narrow passage known as Hell. These remains are now carefully preserved. A monument ascribed to the famous Earl of Pembroke, Richard Strongbow, is placed in the nave. In 1487 Lambert Simnel, the impostor, was crowned here. In mediæval times the cathedral was rich in MSS., shrines and other relics, possessing, among others, a *bachall* or walking-staff, said to have belonged to St. Patrick.

A short walk through a very unsavoury neighbourhood brings the visitor from Christ Church to the Liffey, and immediately before him on the north bank he sees another noted structure—the Four Courts of Dublin, one of the most imposing buildings in the city, and one which, unlike some of the others, has remained true throughout its history to the objects for which it was built. It occupies an oblong, having a frontage on the river of 440 feet. The foundation stone was laid in 1786, it was opened for business in 1797, and it cost about £200,000. It consists of a central block of building, surmounted by a circular lantern and dome, one of the landmarks of the metropolis. This building is flanked by squares connected with each other and with the main entrance by arcades. Each angle of the main building is occupied by one of the superior courts, viz., Chancery, Queen's Bench, Common Pleas, and Exchequer, whence the name of the

INTERIOR OF CHRIST CHURCH, AS RESTORED.

D 2

pile. The centre under the dome is left free for the meeting of lawyers and clients, and all who have business there, or who are drawn thither by curiosity. A description written fifty years ago applies to it to-day : ' The handsome and towering dome lights the great hall of the Courts, an object of just admiration from its chaste and lofty appearance and proportions. During term time it is crowded with lawyers and pickpockets, strangers and stragglers, the fleeced and the fleecing, the hopeful and the hopeless, the anxious and the careless. At such a period of bustle, a visitor, as a Picture of Dublin benevolently forewarns him, "should look to his pockets." '[1]

In the neighbourhood of the splendid square known as Stephen's Green, and of Kildare Street, many of the scientific institutions of Dublin, first-class clubs and hotels cluster together. The Royal Dublin Society, the Museum of Science and Art, the National Gallery of Ireland, and the Royal Irish Academy are in this region. Not long after this book is in the hands of its readers, the handsome and extensive buildings of the New National Museum will be complete, affording room to display many treasures at present inaccessible to the public. Each of the great institutions mentioned above is well worthy of careful attention. It is no disparagement, however, to the rest to say that upon the attention of the stranger the Museum and the Library of the Royal Irish Academy have paramount claims.

This Society was incorporated in 1786 for the study of science, polite literature, and Irish antiquities, and very skilfully and thoroughly have these objects been accomplished, although even more might have been done could they have controlled larger funds. The museum contains a marvellously varied and rich collection of specimens of Irish art, from the earliest period down to comparatively recent date. Naturally the most interesting objects are those either entirely or almost entirely peculiar to Ireland. And among these what are known as *cumdachs*, or book shrines, hold perhaps the chief place. They are rarely met with except in Ireland, and have played no unimportant part in past days. They, like the famous bell shrines, came into existence as the outcome of the reverential affection manifested towards the chief Irish teachers, such as Patrick, Columba, and Molaise by their successors. The old book, the familiar companion of the early missionary, was untouched ; but all that wealth and skill could do was lavished upon the production of a box or shrine in which to preserve so precious a relic. In some cases this box was hermetically sealed, and no superstition was stronger or more universal than the belief that the opening of such a box would be followed by the direst misfortune.

The oldest and in many respects the most interesting specimen of these in the museum is the Domnach Airgid, or the Silver Shrine. This was for many ages preserved as a reliquary near Clones in County Monaghan. Dr. Petrie's conclusions, given to the Royal Irish Academy in 1838, are generally

[1] *Dublin Penny Journal,* i. 143.

accepted as the true history of this ancient relic. He says, ' In its present state this ancient remain appears to have been equally designed as a shrine for the preservation of relics, and of a book ; but the latter was probably its sole original use. Its form is that of an oblong box, nine inches by seven, and five inches in height. This box is composed of three distinct covers, of which the first, or inner one, is of wood—yew ; the second, or middle one, of copper plated with silver ; and the third, or outer one, of silver, plated with gold. In the comparative ages of these several covers there is obviously a great difference. The first may probably be coeval with the manuscript which it was intended to preserve ; the second, in the style of its scroll, or interlaced ornament, indicates a period betwixt the sixth and twelfth centuries ; while the figures in relief, the ornaments, and the letters on the third, or outer cover, leave no doubt of its being the work of the fourteenth century.'

The inscriptions on the outer case show that the Domnach belonged to the monastery of Clones or See of Clogher, and the John O'Karbri by whose permission the cover was made died in 1353. It is also known from the Irish authorities that St. Patrick gave to St. Mac Carthen, who died in 506, a remarkable reliquary. On the death of Mac Carthen, Tigernach, his successor, became the first Bishop and Abbot of Clones, where he built a new church, to which he removed the See of Clogher. This evidence goes, therefore, to prove that the Domnach is the identical reliquary that once belonged to St. Patrick, and that as its original purpose was evidently to contain a book, and it actually does contain a MS., which can be reasonably referred to the age of St. Patrick, there is reason for the belief that this *is* the original MS. Unfortunately, the membranes of the MS. have stuck together, so that it is only with very great difficulty that any separate leaves can be detached. A few of the pages at the beginning of the MS. have been examined, and found to be 'the first chapter of a Latin version of the Gospel of Matthew, in a character not inconsistent with the age to which, on examination, the MS. was assigned by Dr. Petrie.'

The Domnach Airgid is exhibited in the little room on the first floor, into which has been brought together one of the most remarkable antiquarian collections of Europe. It was purchased for a few pounds by Mr. Geo. Smith, who sold it in 1838 for £300 to the Hon. Henry Westenra, who afterwards became Baron Rossmore, and he ultimately presented it to the Academy. The way in which superstition in later ages centred in and upon these early remains is very finely illustrated by Carleton in one of his most vivid and thrilling stories of Irish peasant life, entitled *The Donagh, or the Horse Stealers.* He there shows how the ordeal of having to swear upon the Donagh led to the discovery of crime, depicting at the same time the impression that the mere sight of the relic used to produce upon an assembly of peasants.

In later days these cases were very richly jewelled and adorned with all the resources of wealth and art. Our engraving shows the one that for centuries enclosed a copy of the Gospels believed to have belonged to Molaise or Laserian, of Devenish Island in Lough Erne, a friend and contemporary of Columba. It was made, an inscription tells us, when Cennfailad was abbot, that is, from 1001 to 1025, and consists of plates of bronze, upon which richly ornamented plates of silver are riveted. The illustration reproduces the chief face of the cover, having in the centre a cross contained in a circle, surrounded by the symbols of the four evangelists.

THE CUMDACH, OR CASE OF ST. MOLAISE'S GOSPELS.

In addition to the Domnach Airgid, the Museum possesses another relic which there is good reason for believing dates from the time of St. Patrick, viz., his bell. 'The iron bell of St. Patrick is at once the most authentic and the oldest Irish relic of Christian metal work that has descended to us. It possesses the singular merit of having an unbroken history through 1400 years. This bell is quadrilateral, and is formed of two plates of sheet iron which are bent over so as to meet, and are fastened together by large-headed iron rivets. The corners are rounded by a gentle inclination of the parts which join. One of the plates constitutes the face, the crown and the upper third of the back, as well as the adjacent portion of each side, being doubled over at the top, and descending to meet the smaller plate, which overlaps it at the junction. Subsequently to the securing the joints by rivets, the iron frame was consolidated by the fusion of bronze into the joints and over the surface, giving to the whole a metallic solidity which very much enhanced its resonance, as well as contributed to its preservation. The handle is of iron, let in by projecting spikes to perforations on the ridge of the bell, and further secured on the outside by bronze attachments of its straps.'[1]

This bell belongs to a class of ecclesiastical objects of which numerous specimens have come down to us. Over fifty are extant in Ireland, and they are not uncommon in Wales and Scotland. In the case of St. Patrick's Bell the history can be clearly traced. About the eleventh century it became the custom, out of reverence for the early Christian teachers, to prepare costly and richly jewelled cases or shrines for these bells. We give an engraving of that in which St. Patrick's Bell was for many centuries enshrined. It is a splendid example of goldsmith's work, and it was made between 1091 and 1103, when Donell MacAulay, the name found in the inscription upon it, was Archbishop of Armagh. It is of brass, upon which silver-gilt plates are fastened, and fine gold filigree work; it is adorned with gems and crystal. 'Since it was made, about 1091, it has never been lost sight of.

THE SHRINE OF ST. PATRICK'S BELL.

From the beginning it had a special keeper; in succeeding generations its custody was continued in the same family, and proved to them a source of considerable emolument, and in after ages, when its profits ceased to

_____

[1] *Transactions of the Royal Irish Academy,* 1877.

accrue, long association so bound it up with the affections of the keeper's family that they almost held their existence upon the tenure of its safe custody, and then handed it down from generation to generation, till the stock at last became extinct, and the object of their former care passed into a keeping established by friendship instead of blood.'[1]

From the beginning of the twelfth century until about the commencement of the present, the bell and its shrine was in the custody of a family named Mulholland. The last representative of this family, being childless, entrusted them to the care of the late Adam McLean, Esq., of Belfast. They then passed into the possession of Dr. Todd, from whose executor they were purchased for the Academy for the sum of £500.

It would be possible to fill many pages with descriptions of the beautiful objects contained in this museum, illustrative of the knowledge, skill, and perseverance put forth at a time when many persons fancy that Ireland was inhabited only by hordes of savages, mainly occupied in the slaughter of each other. The museum is crowded with whole classes of specimens of which we can take no note—arms, dress, objects the uses of most of which are known, but in some few cases remain yet undiscovered, illustrative of all epochs of Irish history, and of all classes of people who, during historic and even pre-

THE ARDAGH CHALICE.

historic times, have lived upon Irish soil. In fact, the only museum that equals it in compactness, in devotion to very clearly defined objects, and in comfort to the observer—by which we mean skilful arrangement of contents, combined with the fact that these are not bewildering in number and extent —is the much more widely-known Museum of Northern Antiquities at Copenhagen. All readers of this book who wish to appreciate the past of Ireland should make a point, whenever they visit Dublin, of giving more than a hasty inspection to this treasure-house of the past. Much, however, as we should like to linger, we have space to glance at only three more typical specimens, viz., the Ardagh Chalice, the Tara Brooch, and the Cross of Cong.

The gem of the whole collection, and in many respects one of the most beautiful and noteworthy objects in Europe, is the Ardagh Chalice.

[1] *Early Christian Art in Ireland*, p. 59.

When it was made no evidence is extant to show, but all judges agree
that at the very least it is over 1000 years old.   It was found, with other
specimens of Celtic art, by a lad digging potatoes in a *rath* or early fort
near the village of Ardagh in Co. Limerick.   It belongs to the class of
cups known as *calices ministrales*, in use before the tenth century, intended
for the use of the minor clergy and laity, before the Roman Catholic
Church debarred the laity from the communion in both kinds.

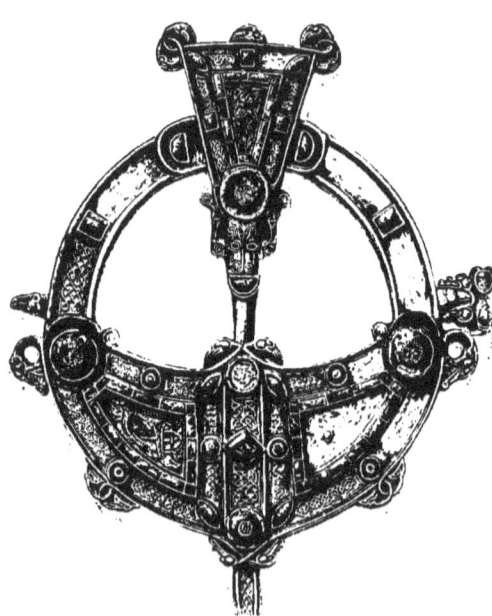

The chalice is com-
posed of an alloy of
silver, is seven inches
high, nine and a half
inches in diameter, the
bowl being four inches
deep.   In the various
parts, no less than 354
in number, gold, silver,
bronze, brass, copper
and lead, are used.   The
upper rim is of brass,
much decayed and split
from some local action
on that particular kind
of alloy.   The bowl is
of silver, the standard
value of which is four
shillings to the ounce.
The ornaments cut on
the silver bowl consist
of an inscription, inter-
laced patterns terminat-
ing in dogs' heads, and
at the bottom a circular
band of the Greek pat-
tern.   The mode of
ornamentation is peculiar to this cup, being done with a chisel and hammer.
Round the cup runs a band composed of two semi-cylindrical rings of silver
ornamented with small annular dots punched out with a hollow punch.
The space between the rings is filled with twelve plaques of gold *repoussé*
work with a very beautiful ornamentation of fine filigree wirework, wrought
on the front of the *repoussé* ground, and carrying out in its most delicate
execution the interlaced pattern associated with the art of the country.
Between the plaques are twelve round enamelled beads.[1]

THE TARA BROOCH (OBVERSE).

[1] *Early Christian Art in Ireland*, p. 81.

Although the object is so small, there are no less than forty different designs discoverable in its decorative work. A well-preserved inscription is engraved on the cup containing the names of the twelve apostles as given in the Romish Canon of the Mass.

The Tara Brooch, in the general character and exquisite style of its ornamentation, belongs to the same period of art as the Ardagh Chalice. It was found in 1850, near the sea-shore, by the child of a poor woman, who afterwards sold it in Drogheda. The workmanship is so highly finished that to be fairly appreciated it should be examined through a powerful lens. It exhibits seventy-six varieties of design, of the class found in the Ardagh Chalice and the early illuminated Irish MSS. The obverse and reverse are both richly decorated. 'The Tara Brooch,' said Dr. Petrie, 'is superior to anything hitherto found in the variety of its ornaments and in the exquisite delicacy and perfection of its execution.' It is composed of what is known as white bronze, a mixture of copper and tin.

The Ardagh Chalice deposed what is known

THE TARA BROOCH (REVERSE).

as the Cross of Cong from the proud position of chief among the works of art in the museum. This is a famous relic, dating from the Middle Ages, enshrining and illustrating, as so many of the articles in this fascinating building do, the traditions and habits and life of the early Irish Church. This cross was constructed, as one of the five inscriptions upon it states, for the following purpose: 'In this cross is preserved the cross on which the Founder of the world suffered.' In other words, it is a reliquary, and at one time was believed to contain a piece of the cross upon which Jesus Christ suffered 'the just for the unjust,' in order 'that He should gather together in one the children of God that were scattered abroad.' It was made by order of Turlough O'Connor, father of the last king who ruled Ireland prior to the Norman invasion, about the year 1123, and placed in the Church of Tuam,

THE CROSS OF CONG.

during the Archbishopric of Muiredach O'Duffy, who died in 1150. This is clearly shown by the inscriptions still de-cipherable upon it. It was transferred to Cong either by O'Duffy, who died there, or by order of King Turlough O'Con-nor, who founded and endowed that abbey. At the time of the Reformation it was con-cealed in an oaken chest, and early in the present century a parish priest, the Rev. Mr. Prendergast, found chest and relic in a cottage. From his successor Professor MacCul-lagh bought it, and presented it to the Museum.

The shaft is thirty in-ches high, the arms eighteen and three-quarter in-ches broad, and it is one and three-quarter in-ches thick. It is of oak, covered with plates of copper. On the central plate of the front at the junction of the cross is a large crystal, through which what was supposed to be the true cross could be seen. Eighteen jewels were placed at regular intervals, and of these thirteen still remain. Two out of the four beads which origin-ally surrounded the central boss remain. The lower part of the shaft is the head of a grotesque animal, beneath which is the richly decorated ball containing the socket into which the pole was inserted by which the reliquary was borne aloft on processional occasions.

Coming back from this remote past, we must glance at a few other points of special note before we leave Dublin for the country. Of Dublin Castle we need only say that there is nothing very special to be said about it. It possesses few noteworthy features of anti-quarian or architectural in-terest. The Chapel Royal is a work of high artistic character, and well repays a visit. Its sculpture is fine, and of a high class. The Bermingham Tower is of considerable age and interest. It contains valuable State papers, and was formerly used as a State prison. What importance attaches to the Castle now arises mainly from the fact that it has long been the centre and the symbol of England's authority over Ireland.

Dublin is favoured with suburbs that are easily accessible, beautiful in their scenery, and rich in historical and antiquarian associations. It is in this connection, although it hardly comes under the description of a suburb, that reference must be made to Phœnix Park. The name has no reference to the ancient fable, but is derived from *fionn uisge*, clear or limpid water, the name originally given to a beautiful spring near the Phœnix Pillar. This being pronounced 'feenisk,' was easily corrupted into Phœnix. The park was seized by the Crown on the suppression of the Knights Templars, whose residence was at Kilmainham, and who owned the land on both sides of the Liffey. It is a magnificent piece of country, seven miles in circuit, with an area of 1760 acres. It is well wooded, undulating in parts, with many level open spaces, in which hurling, football, and other games are eagerly played by the youth of Dublin ; and, from different points of vantage, very fine views are obtained. Within its limits stand the Viceregal Lodge, the houses of the Chief and the Under-Secretaries for Ireland, a military school and infirmary, a large constabulary barracks, and the building in which the Ordnance Survey work is carried on. It also contains a review ground, a People's Gardens, and a Zoological Gardens. The military prowess of Ireland is commemorated here by an imposing, if not beautiful, obelisk to Wellington and a statue to Lord Gough.

The Botanic Gardens at Glasnevin, hard by the large cemetery in which the modern round tower in memory of O'Connell rises to a great height, are also very lovely, well kept, and so laid out as to enable the frequenter easily and considerably to increase his knowledge of flowers and shrubs. The Curator's house was once the abode of the poet Tickell, and a grove of aged yew trees is still known as 'Addison's Walk.' No place could well be prettier, or more attractive to a lover of botany than Glasnevin on a fine afternoon in early summer.

Needing a somewhat longer journey, and yet within easy reach, are Clontarf and Howth, Clondalkin, Kingstown, and Killiney. All of these are much frequented by the residents of Dublin. Clontarf is midway between Dublin and Howth, and was the scene of that famous battle fought on Good Friday, 1014, between Brian Borumha and the Danes under Sihtric. The Danes were defeated and their power broken, but the chieftain who has ever since stood out as the typical Irish monarch was slain. Brian became King of Munster in 976, he established his power over the whole of Ireland in 1002. He was able and strong in war, wise in counsel, and not unmindful of the works of peace. 'He erected or restored the cathedral of Killaloe, the churches of Inis-caltra in Lough Derg, the round tower of Tomgraney in County Clare. He built bridges over the Shannon at Athlone and Lanesborough, he constructed roads, he strengthened the forts and island fortresses of Munster. He dispensed a royal hospitality, he administered rigid and impartial justice, and established peace and order through all the country, so that, as the historian puts it, "a woman might walk in safety through the length of Ireland, from Tory Island in Donegal to Glandore Harbour in Cork, carrying a ring of gold on a horse-rod."'[1]

Dr. Stokes, in the book from which we have just quoted, gives a very clear and realistic sketch of the famous battle. It was 'fought all over the ground now occupied by the north side of Dublin, from the wood of Clontarf to the site of the present Four Courts, where stood the only bridge then spanning the river Liffey. It began early in the morning, at sunrise, soon after five o'clock. A strong north-east wind was blowing, as the inhabitants of Dublin still so often experience in April, to their bitter cost. The Danish inhabitants of Dublin crowded the walls of the town, which clustered thick round the hill now crowned by Christ Church Cathedral, whence a splendid view of the fight presented itself. . . . It was a thoroughly Celtic fight, without any skill or plan or manœuvres, consisting merely of a series of individual encounters, which are told in a very Homeric style. . . . The Raven Standard ever fluttered in front of Sigurd, who carried destruction with him wherever he went.'

Sigurd is at length slain by Morrogh O'Brian, the Irish leader, who in turn is mortally wounded by a Dane named Eric, whom Morrogh slays just before he expires. The Danes are then utterly routed, and multitudes perish in trying to reach their ships on the beach at Clontarf. But in the hour of victory came the worst blow to the Irish. Some of the Danes had fled to the woods which covered the heights around Dublin. 'Brian had taken his station on one of these hills to engage in prayer, like Moses, attended by only a few servants. The king was seated on a fur rug, where he prolonged his petitions from early morning till the afternoon, receiving occasional reports concerning the progress of the battle from Latean, his attendant. As the sun began to descend towards the west, the apostate deacon Brodar and two other warriors approached the king's station, seeking refuge in the woods. One of the three had been in Brian's service, and he called Brodar's attention to Brian. "The king, the king!" said he. "No, no, a priest, a priest!" replied Brodar. "By no means," said the soldier; "that is the great King Brian." Brodar then turned round with a battle-axe in his hand. The aged king gathered his remaining strength, aimed a blow at Brodar, which wounded his legs, while Brodar cleft Brian's head in twain. He then continued his flight to the woods, but was shortly afterwards taken and slain. Malachey, King of Meath, who had remained in reserve, now advanced upon the field and completed the work, routing the enemy on every side, thus terminating the domination, though not the presence, of the Danes in Ireland.'[2]

Thus passed away King Brian Boru, in the hour of his final victory. And now, every few minutes, tramcars start from the Nelson Pillar, which

[1] *Ireland and the Celtic Church*, p. 291.   [2] *Ibid.* pp. 302-305.

speedily carry the curious traveller over the plain where the beaten Danes fled in the vain hope of making good their escape in the ships which had so often carried bloodshed and terror around the Irish coasts. A curious proof of the accuracy of the old Irish Annals has been brought to light by modern science. The early accounts of the battle represent the tide as being at its flood at the time of the rout, viz., about 6 o'clock; and Dr. Haughton has proved that on April 23rd, 1014, it was high water in Dublin Bay at 5.55 P.M.

Passing Clontarf, the traveller reaches the Hill of Howth, not only the most prominent feature in the scenery of Dublin Bay, but also a spot rich in antiquities and in the fine views to be obtained from it. Here is the ancient port of Dublin. Here the old Norse sea-rovers used to collect prior to one of their marauding expeditions. Hard by the harbour stand the considerable ruins of the fine old abbey. Beyond that is situated the castle, which is still a fine residence, with very beautiful grounds. Near the Carrigmore cliffs stands a splendid cromlech, consisting of ten huge masses of rock, the one forming the table measuring in one direction eighteen feet, in the other nineteen and a half, having an extreme thickness of eight feet. Continuing the walk round the headland, the well-known Bailey light comes into view, and in completing the circuit fine views of Dublin and the Wicklow Hills delight the eye.

The chief interest of Howth is its lighthouse, with the wonderful gas-light beacon of Mr. Wigham, which has revolutionized the old system of using oil lamps for lighthouse illumination. According to the depth of fog and atmospheric opacity, additional supplies of light are available without delay, and a penetrating power, hitherto undreamed of, at once supplied.

CHAPTER II.

THE GARDEN OF IRELAND.

FEW capitals are richer in pretty and picturesque scenery close at hand than Dublin. Still fewer possess in addition wide tracts of exceedingly lovely country so close that almost all of the best parts can easily be visited in a day's picnic. The inhabitant of Dublin need be at no loss how or where to enjoy himself when he snatches a holiday from the ordinary routine of daily work. The counties of Wicklow and Wexford present an almost embarrassing choice of delightful excursions.

He has only to take the train, and in a few minutes he is at Kingstown, a fashionable suburb of the great city. This is a modern place, and owes much of its importance to the fact that the mail traffic between Dublin and Holyhead passes through it. Large hotels have been built here; there are multitudes of well-kept villas, and it has become a fashionable resort for well-to-do merchants and people of leisure. Kingstown during the summer gives itself up to music and promenading, to bathing and lounging, to yachting and the never-failing delight of watching the mail packets come and go. The land rises abruptly from the harbour, enabling the place to look beautiful under the white light of day, and even more beautiful under the subdued glow of the many lights dotted about the hilly streets and lanes.

The favourite excursion in the immediate neighbourhood of Kingstown is

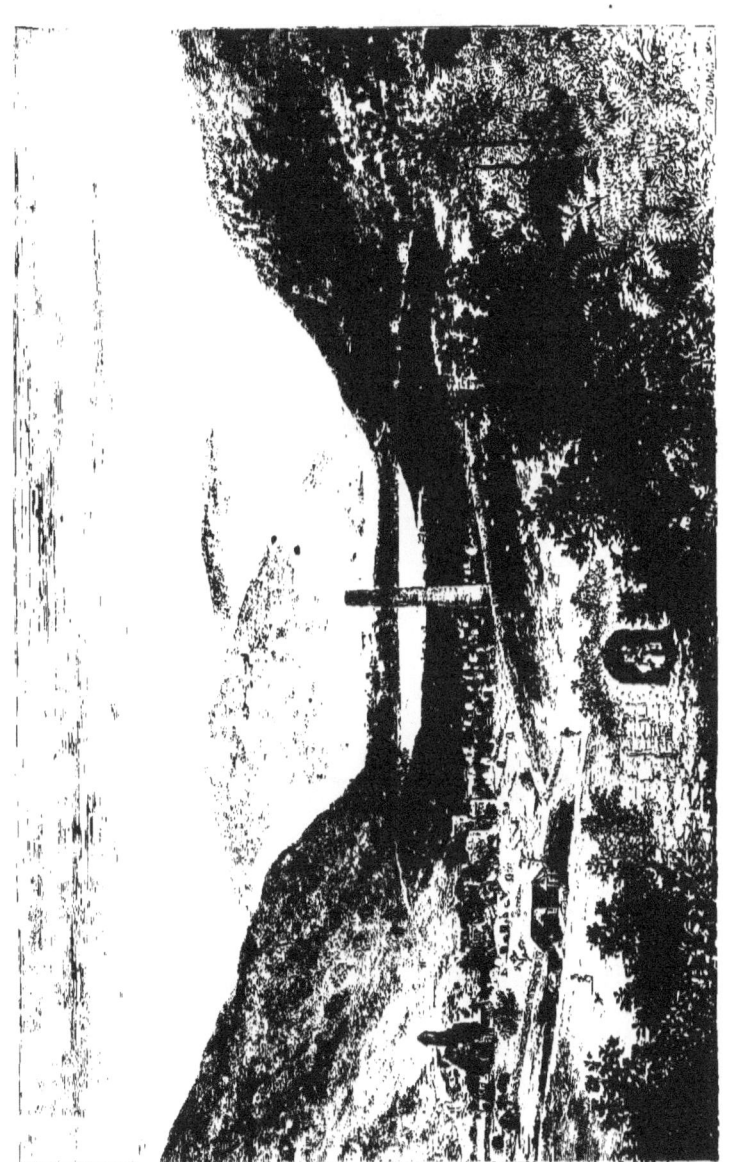

The Vale of Glendalough.

the walk to the top of Killiney, a bold hill rising to the height of 480 feet. Enthusiastic residents occasionally affirm that the view from the top of this on a fine clear day has no rival in Europe; and although the traveller may not always see his way to the acceptance of this conclusion, he will readily admit that it is impossible to get a lovelier view at so little cost in the way of exertion.

A still more fashionable summer resort is Bray. This place is even younger than Kingstown, having been quite unknown until comparatively recent times. Fifty years ago it was occupied by a few fishermen's huts; now it is crowded with enormous hotels, fine private residences, and all the signs

SUGAR-LOAF MOUNTAIN.

of a considerable resident population. Fifty years ago the shore was a lonely beach; now it is a magnificent esplanade, extending along the water's edge, backed by spacious villas and supplied with baths, pleasure-gardens, and all the devices calculated to attract and detain those who like to combine the comforts of a big town with the advantages of sea-air and sea-bathing.

Rising abruptly to the south, is the Bri or Bree, meaning 'headland,' whence comes its name. This has been tunnelled by the railway, and so laid out that the walk around the face of the promontory affords a varied series of delightful views. In the height of the season Bray is very lively, and all those phases of life which have been developed by the modern

E 2

fondness for fashionable sea-side summer life can here be studied by means
of numerous examples.

But Bray is only at the gate of the beauties of Wicklow; and within certain
limits the further afield one travels the richer is the reward, if the traveller
be a lover of nature, and in sympathy with what has been most worthy in the
past. Much that is very pretty in the immediate neighbourhood of Bray is
somewhat vulgarized by the nearness of that centre of fashionable idleness.
It is when the traveller gets twenty or thirty miles away that he enters into
the full enjoyment of a really lovely region, where the tired worker, the
overtaxed, the student, the man or woman brought below physical par by
stress and strain of life, or by the partial breakdown of bodily and nervous
power, may regain elasticity for the mind, tone for the nervous system, and

THE DARGLE.

restoration of bodily
vigour. Few could
spend their holidays
in visiting Sugar-
loaf Mountain,
Glendalough, the
Vale of Ovoca,
Glenmalure, and a
dozen other beauti-
ful adjacent dis-
tricts without being
the better physically
and mentally, and
without increasing
their love for na-
tural beauty.

To begin with
the things nearest
to Bray. No visitor
is long at a loss as to what objects are to be seen, or how he may
see them. At every turn car-drivers, hackney coachmen, and guides
offer to conduct you to the Dargle, to the Glen of Downs, to Powerscourt Waterfall, or where you will, within a radius of ten or fifteen
miles. The most popular excursion is to the Dargle and Powerscourt.
The former is a beautiful little mountain glen, well wooded, kindly furnished
by nature with that usual high rock from which fable insists upon hurling
the usual unhappy lover. Like many other much frequented spots, the
reputation of the Dargle sometimes suffers from the extravagant praises of
those who admire it 'not wisely but too well.' The bridge is a favourite
spot not only for the lover of the beautiful, but also a starting-place for
the angler. The origin of the name is a subject of controversy. Some

maintain that it comes from the Celtic *Daur Glin*, or Vale of Oaks; but Dr. Joyce, on the other hand, maintains that it comes from an Irish word *dearg*, meaning 'red,' and that *Deargail*, now Dargle, means 'a red little spot.' He fortifies his view by saying: 'I have on other occasions observed how happily the old name-formers generally succeeded in designating places by their most obvious characteristics, every name striking straight for the feature that most strongly attracted attention, so that to this day a person moderately skilled in such matters may often predict the physical peculiarities or the aspect of a place as soon as he hears the name. Nothing could be more appropriate in this respect than the Dargle, which everyone will recognize as the name of a beautiful glen near Bray in Wicklow. The prevailing rock in the glen is very soft and of a reddish colour, sometimes with a yellowish tinge, but in several places deepening into a dark purplish red. The visitor can hardly fail to observe this almost as soon as he enters the lower gate, where the red stones come to the surface of the path under his feet. The reddish colour also pervades the clay, which is merely the rock worn down; and is very striking in several spots along the sides of the glen, where the clay and the rock are exposed, especially after rain, which brings out the prevailing hue very vividly.'[1]

POWERSCOURT WATERFALL.

Near the head of the glen is the well-situated village of Enniskerry, and after a drive of a few miles through Lord Powerscourt's property, the Powerscourt Waterfall is reached. This again is very pretty, although occasionally visitors are disappointed, because somewhat overdrawn descrip-

[1] *Irish Names of Places*, ii. 39.

tions have raised their expectations too high. The effectiveness of the fall necessarily varies with the body of water coming over it. It is a fine fall and picturesquely situated ; but he who goes fancying it is as picturesque as the Kilefos in the Naerödal, or as voluminous as the Mongefos in the Romsdal, will assuredly be disappointed, no matter how heavily it may have rained just prior to his visit.

A good pedestrian can make this the starting-point for a trip among the Wicklow Mountains, several of the highest peaks being in the neighbourhood, the highest mountain being Kippure, which just succeeds in

POWERSCOURT HOUSE.

From a photograph by Lawrence of Dublin.

overtopping the Donegal Errigal, and reaches an altitude of 2,475 feet. These do not seem very lofty in comparison with the Alpine giants, but they are quite high enough to afford healthy exercise and many splendid prospects.

A very fine drive is to continue on from the waterfall along Glencree to the Upper and Lower Lough Bray, 1,453 feet above the sea, nestling at the foot of Kippure, and then return by way of Enniskerry. Any one wishful to see a good specimen of a fine Irish country residence can gratify his taste by visiting Powerscourt House. It is more remarkable for extent

and beauty of situation than for exceptional excellence in architecture.
Powerscourt demesne covers about 26,000 acres. The first English owner
was De la Poer, one of Strongbow's companions. The O'Byrnes and
O'Tooles of Wicklow captured it in Henry VIII.'s time, and when retaken
it was bestowed upon the Talbots. In 1556 the Kavanaghs acquired
possession of it; and in 1608 James I. bestowed it upon Sir R.
Wingfield, who was created Viscount Powerscourt in 1618.

On the road from Enniskerry to Dublin, and within an easy
drive of Bray, is a wild ravine known as the Scalp. The road
runs over a shoulder of Shankhill Mountain and through this
ravine; it presents a very wild appearance, enormous masses
of granite being heaped up in grand and picturesque confusion
on either side. It looks as if nature, in order to spare man
the trouble of blasting a road, had by some mighty
convulsion torn a rent through the mountain just wide

THE SCALP.

enough for a high road. Professor Hill has shown that the Scalp was once the channel of a great river that drained districts of land, now denuded of extensive rock deposits, and which discharged itself through the Irish Sea in distant ages. From the south entrance a very fine view is obtained, having in the foreground the Greater and the Lesser Sugar Loaf Mountains.

Another pleasant trip is along the road which skirts the foot of the Great Sugar Loaf Mountain, passing through the Glen of Downs, another of these lovely Wicklow dells. It consists of a deep, well-wooded ravine, the banks at some points rising to a height of 800 feet. The road runs to Delgany, whence the return to Bray is direct.

But, as we have already suggested, he who would rightly appreciate the scenery of this part of Ireland must go somewhat further afield. In the central and southern part of Wicklow are to be found the finest examples both of the softer and lovely country, and also of the sterner, gloomy and wild mountain scenery. The centre towards which all excursions in this region tend by a very natural attraction is the Vale of Glendalough ; and the reason for this is not far to seek. It is one of the loveliest spots upon which the eye can rest. It is associated, like so many other beautiful parts of Ireland, with the past history and religious life of the nation ; and the national tendency to associate romance and tragedy with exceptional natural features is well illustrated here.

Glendalough is a mountain valley, situated, fortunately, in the opinion of the lover of nature, some miles from the nearest railway station. It is shut in on every side, except the east, by mountains, and starting from it several smaller valleys run up into the hills on either side. Two lakes lie embosomed in the valley, and looking towards the upper end from the eastern entrance it appears to be entirely enclosed by abrupt and lofty mountains. To the east of the lakes, situated in the centre of the valley, is a remarkable cluster of ancient buildings—a round tower, early Irish churches, one nearly perfect, others in ruins, the remains of an ancient cathedral, an early cross, and a considerable number of old and modern tombstones. The buildings clustered at this spot, together with others scattered over the valley, make up the far-famed Seven Churches of Glendalough.

But before we enter into fuller detail, it may be well to glance at the various ways of reaching this valley. If Bray is the starting-point, Rathnew is the nearest station, and the pedestrian will find it an agreeable walk to go by way of the Devil's Glen and the Roundwood Reservoir. Those not equal to a ten or fifteen mile stretch can ride to the Glen, walk up that, and regain their car at the top. Approached from the south, Rathdrum is the station, and then the visitor has a walk or drive of about ten miles through most delightful country. We should be disposed to recommend Rathdrum as the starting-point. As there is a capital hotel at Glendalough, and as the country is admirably suited for walking, the visitor with time and strength at his disposal need not choose the shortest road, but may reach the Seven Churches by way of the Military Road and Glenmalure. This road is a measure of the difficulties that have been experienced in the past in the government of these districts. It was built during the troubles of 1798 to facilitate the movements of troops in this region; it remains as a boon to the adventurous and scenery-loving traveller. Glenmalure is one of the finest of Wicklow valleys, and when at Drumgoff, where the road from Rathdrum joins the Military Road, the traveller can easily, if he wishes, obtain a guide and make the ascent of Lugnaquilla, the highest mountain in Wicklow, 3,039 feet. The view from the summit, over Wexford, Waterford, and Cork, is very extensive.

But the great majority prefer the beaten path; that which runs by the Vale of Clara to Laragh. And much beyond the fact that it is the shorter and more convenient may be said for this route; as a drive it is not easy to find its equal. Rathdrum occupies a lovely situation on the Avonmore River, at the junction of two valleys; through one of these comes the railroad from Wexford, and along the other runs the road to Glendalough. The whole drive to Laragh is a succession of beautiful views, the road following the Vale of Clara, the Avonmore river being almost always in sight, and usually at a great distance below the traveller; the slopes of the hills are richly wooded. At Laragh the road turns abruptly to the west, and very soon traces of the manifold remains of ancient buildings, which abound in this region, begin to appear. The road skirts the northern bank of a little stream, at a considerable elevation above it. On the southern bank, about a mile from Laragh, are the ruins known as the Priory of St. Saviour's, probably the site of an ancient monastery, and, according to some, of the ancient religious town of Glendalough. The remains are scanty, but they exhibit many curious specimens of Irish ornamental carving of the ninth and tenth centuries. A few yards from the road, nearly opposite the Priory, stand the walls of a tiny structure known as Trinity Church. It belongs to a very early period, and exhibits fine examples of a square-headed doorway, a choir arch and chancel windows.

Shortly after passing this church, the Vale of Glendalough comes into sight, and presents on a fine day one of the most beautiful pictures that the 'Garden of Ireland' can show. To the right is the Vale of Glendasan, to the left Glendalough; a mountain juts out boldly to a well-defined edge, separating the two valleys, and in the distance are clearly seen the mountains that shut in the upper end of the valley. If the visitor is driving it is customary to take him up to the western end of the valley, by the shores of the upper lake, and leave him to explore the beauties and antiquities of that region, and then walk down again to the cashel. By these shores St. Kevin, the founder of the first ecclesiastical buildings erected here, lived his hermit life. The saint is an undoubtedly historical character, and flourished

in the early part of the sixth century. The facts seem to be that he built
the cell on the south shore of the lake, known as Tempul-na-skellig, also
part of the building known as St. Kevin's Kitchen, and that he lived for
years in the vale ; but as usual legend has been very busy with his name.
Once when the saint, according to his habit, extended his hand from the
window of his cell in the attitude of supplication, a blackbird dropped her
eggs into it. He never altered the position, hand or arm, until the
eggs were hatched ! It was by these lakes that King O'Toole, when too
old to hunt, used to amuse himself by watching his geese swim. Great was
his grief when his favourite gander became too old to fly. To him comes
the saint, 'What will you give me if I make him fly again for you?'
'Why, I'll give you all the ground he flies over, even suppose he flew
round the whole glen.' With that exactness always noticeable on these
occasions, the gander *did* fly round the whole glen. ' Now,' said the saint,
' King O'Toole, be as good as your word, give me this place, and I will
dedicate it to God.' And King O'Toole, 'putting a handsome face on it,'
made over the valley for ever and a day to the enterprising saint.

The savage side of asceticism, and its unnatural violation of the duties
and claims of ordinary life, are illustrated by the legend of Kathleen. To
escape from her affectionate entreaties, the saint fled to the hole in the cliff
overhanging the upper lake, up to which tourists occasionally climb, under-
going thus needless risks, to the enrichment of the wily boatmen and
guides. But the saint's hopes of peace were vain. Even here Kathleen
found him.

> Fearless she had tracked his feet.
> To this rocky wild retreat !
> And when morning met his view,
> Her mild glances met it too.
>
> Ah ! you saints have cruel hearts !
> Sternly from his bed he starts,
> And with rude repulsive shock,
> Hurls her from the beetling rock.

That such a legend could be told, as it undoubtedly was, to the saint's
credit, is but one of manifold proofs that a too exclusive and mistaken
notion about the salvation of one's own soul may lead to extraordinary
callousness as to the rights of others, and the claims of mercy. But
St. Kevin is not responsible for the foolish legends that have centred about
his personality. To him belongs whatever credit is due for the foundation of
an ecclesiastical establishment at Glendalough. Later generations extended
and developed his work.

In the immediate neighbourhood of the eastern end of the upper lake
are the remains of what is now called Refeart or Refeert Church, dating
from St. Kevin's time, and exhibiting still a fine specimen of a very ancient

doorway. It was here, according to tradition, that King O'Toole was buried.

There is a fine walk along the southern edge of the valley from the upper lake to the main cluster of ancient buildings. These are all enclosed in a cashel or wall, entered through a fine old gateway, which was standing forty years ago, and which, having fallen down since, was restored and securely rebuilt some years ago, the same stones being used and replaced as far as possible in their original order. The structures of note here are St. Kevin's Kitchen, the Lady Chapel, the Cathedral and the Round Tower. Of these the first is, at any rate in part, contemporaneous with the saint. It once consisted of a nave and chancel, with a sacristy at the east end and a belfry at the west. The chancel has disappeared; the other parts remain. Of these the nave only dates from the sixth century. It is called the Kitchen from the absurd notion, once prevalent, that the belfry was a chimney! Divested of the turret and the sacristy, the building resembles somewhat St. Columbkille's house at Kells. It is nearly thirty feet long, twenty-two feet wide, and the walls are three feet seven inches thick. Its side walls are eleven feet high, and the ridge of the roof thirty-one feet above the ground. The belfry and sacristy are later additions when the building was used as a church. Dr. Petrie sees no reason to doubt that 'this building, in its original state, was at once the habitation and the oratory of the eminent ecclesiastic to whom the religious establishment at Glendalough owed its origin; and it is highly probable that it received, shortly after his death, those additions which were necessary to make it a church, fit for the worship of those who would be led thither from reverence to his name.'[1]

The Round Tower is very ancient, dating most probably from about the tenth century. It is well built, but, like several others, has lost its original roof and some of the upper courses. These have been restored in recent years, and a conical roof having been added, the tower presents much the same appearance as it must have done originally. The doorway is now about ten feet from the ground, and was probably originally fifteen feet, there having been in the course of centuries an accumulation of debris around its base. In the engraving on page 49 the tower is depicted as it was prior to the restoration of the roof.

The small church, erroneously called now the Church of Our Lady, is, in the opinion of Dr. Petrie, contemporary with St. Kevin's House. The Cathedral—a somewhat ambitious name for so small a structure—is roofless. The nave is very ancient, and the west door is a fine specimen of one of the earliest types of ecclesiastical architecture. The chancel is somewhat later in style, and therefore in date. Even if we cannot accept the earlier date, although there seems no sufficient reason to doubt it, the storms of

[1] *The Round Towers of Ireland*, p. 435.

nearly a thousand years, and all the mischances and ravages of thirty generations, have failed to destroy these examples of Irish piety and skill.

But with many the interest of their visit to Glendalough depends but slightly upon these architectural treasures. They go for the exhilaration of the tramp or the ride; they delight in the bold hill contours, in the peaceful lakes, in the smiling valley, in the wooded slopes. And these are sufficient reasons. He who can traverse the rich and varied country encircling the valley, or ramble along its pleasant paths without being the better for it, is not to be envied. And yet it must be admitted that some due appreciation of the relative antiquity of the various remains, of the part they have played in religious history, of the testimony they bear to the zeal, industry, faith and skill of past generations—all the more powerful because this can neither flatter nor deceive—greatly heightens the pleasure and increases the benefit of such a visit.

On a bright summer day here, as at Clonmacnois, at Cashel, at Slane, there is the blending of the fresh and lovely present with the dim, yet no less real, past. The air, the sky, the face of nature, the contour of the mountains are much the same to us as they were to St. Kevin; but as we pace the unroofed nave of the cathedral, or stand in the shadow of the lofty tower, or try to decipher the sculptures on an ancient cross; as we think of the successive generations of Celt and Saxon that have passed away whilst these relics of human skill have survived, of the fierce Northmen who again and again ravaged the valley, of the long struggle that raged for the possession of these fair regions, there comes upon us that pleasant emotion, due in part to facts and in part to imagination, the sense of satisfaction that we are able to see, mark, and ponder over the works of other ages, surviving in a natural setting, which is at once ever old and ever new.

The traveller who has reached Glendalough from Rathdrum will find it pleasant to return by way of Roundwood and the Devil's Glen. The drive to the former is not so interesting as that through the Vale of Clara, but the walk along the great reservoir of the Vartry that supplies Dublin is worth a visit. This reservoir is an artificial lough, with an area of 400 acres, and formed by a huge dam 1,600 feet long, 40 feet wide at the base and 30 at the top. It can supply the metropolis at the rate of 12,000,000 gallons a day. The water travels twenty-four miles through pipes ere it reaches those who use it.

Near to the Vartry reservoir is a road leading to the head of the Devil's Glen. This is a very fine wooded glen about two miles long, through which the Vartry flows. Entering from the upper end, the finest scenery is met first. The glen is closed by abrupt ledges of rock, and over these the river tumbles and roars in a succession of fine falls. Cars are not allowed to drive through, and so those who wish to see the beauties

THE VALE OF AVOCA.

must perforce walk.   It is well worth the trouble.   Rock scenery is the chief feature of the glen.   It was a prominent place in the 1798 rebellion, and was for a time one of the strongholds of the famous Wicklow general, Holt.

The road from the Devil's Glen through Rathnew to Wicklow has many pleasant spots, though at neither place is there anything of special interest.   The 'Garden of Ireland' extends further to the south and west, and below Rathdrum is situated its most celebrated district, the Vale of Avoca or Ovoca, since it seems to answer to both names.   This is a lovely valley through which the Avonmore flows, until it meets and mingles its waters with the Avonbeg.   The spot where the union takes place is known as the Meeting of the Waters, and it is difficult to conceive of lovelier scenery.   On a sunny summer's day the visitor feels that the United Kingdom cannot show a fairer scene.   Still even here man has done what he can to mar the beauty.   The railway—a necessary evil—runs through it; yet as it is only a single line and trains are not frequent, this is not such a drawback as it might be.   But between Rathdrum and Gorey great beds of copper-pyrites exist, and were recently being worked, and the result, while probably satisfactory from the commercial point of view, has been disastrous to the picturesque effect.   The great heaps of reddish-brown refuse seem sadly out of place.   The associations and evidences of mining come upon one as a painful contrast, when suddenly encountered in the midst of so much pure loveliness.   Doubtless some of the popularity of this region is due to Moore's verses; but then his lines do fairly represent the impression produced upon a sympathetic observer by the quiet beauty of these peaceful scenes. Allowing something for Celtic imagination, the description even yet holds good :

'There is not in this wide world a valley so sweet
As the vale in whose bosom the bright waters meet;
Oh! the last rays of feeling and life must depart
Ere the bloom of that valley shall fade from my heart.

Yet, it was not that Nature had shed o'er the scene
Her purest of crystal, and brightest of green;
'Twas not the soft magic of streamlet or hill,
Oh, no! it was something more exquisite still.

'Twas that friends, the beloved of my bosom, were near,
Who made each dear scene of enchantment more dear;
And who felt how the best charms of Nature improve
When we see them reflected from looks that we love.

Sweet Vale of Avoca! how calm could I rest
In thy bosom of shade with the friends I love best,
Where the storms that we feel in this cold world should cease,
And our hearts, like thy waters, be mingled in peace.'

A few miles south-west of Wooden Bridge Station is the wood of Shillelagh, famous as having given the name to that weapon with which so many Irish heads have been broken in past days. But as long ago as 1693 the greater part of the wood was cut down for use in the furnaces of the ironworks of that period. Westminster Hall is said to have been roofed with oak cut from the woods of Shillelagh.

The railroad from Wooden Bridge to Wexford passes through a country which, if not quite equal to the Vale of Avoca, yet presents much to charm the eye. Wexford itself is a quaint, busy little seaport, inseparably associated with Oliver Cromwell, by reason of the terrible assault and capture in 1649, and interesting to the stranger now. It has also unhappy memories connected with the outbreak of 1798. The massacre on the Bridge of Wexford, and the Battle of Vinegar Hill, testify both to the passionate desire on the part of the insurgents to throw off the English yoke, and to the stern suppression of the rising by the Government of that day. Like its neighbour Waterford, Wexford owes its foundation to the Danes, and commemorates that fact in its name.

The town of New Ross and the city of Waterford are both well worth a visit. The sail along the Barrow from the one to the other is very enjoyable, and at the junction with the Suir a fine view of Dunbrody Abbey is obtained. The approach to Waterford from the sea is striking. As the Milford Haven steamer draws near the entrance to Waterford Harbour, Hook Head, with its prominent lighthouse, juts boldly out into the sea. A few miles to the north-east another promontory can be seen, known as Bag-an-bun Head. On the Hook Head side of this, in the year 1169, Robert Fitzstephen and his companions landed, and began that long strife between English and Irish which has not ceased although nearly seven hundred years have passed since, to use the rhyming legend that has become current— 'At Bag-an-bun Ireland was lost and won.'

Waterford is the chief port of South-eastern Ireland, and a great centre of the cattle trade. It is prettily situated on the Suir, the quays stretching for over a mile along the south bank of that river. But it must be admitted that its claims upon the traveller's attention are soon exhausted, however engrossing they may be upon the man of business. The only structure in it that presents a somewhat ancient appearance is Reginald's Tower, on the quay, and this can hardly make good its claim to an existence of over eight hundred years.

DROGHEDA FROM THE RAILWAY BRIDGE.

CHAPTER III.

THE VALLEY OF THE BOYNE.

'THE Garden of Ireland,' as it is popularly called, lies to the south of Dublin. But this descriptive phrase applies with almost equal force to the region lying immediately to the north of the metropolis. Few districts in the kingdom can show so much lovely scenery, and into no part of it are compressed so many ancient sites, ruined castles, fine old churches and abbeys, and famous battle-fields. The stretch of country drained by the Boyne and the Blackwater has been renowned in Irish story from the dawn of history until the present day. Here is the great cemetery of the ancient pagan kings who flourished before the earliest Irish scribe began to pen the annals of his country; here stands the Hill of Tara, yet evidencing, by its clearly traceable signs, the barbaric splendour of King Laoghaire's Court; here is the Hill of Slane, upon which St. Patrick kindled that Easter light, the outward symbol of the spiritual light which more or less brightly has never ceased to shine in the Sacred Isle; here stood the ancient kingdom of Meath; and with every square mile of the country is connected some deed of daring or of cruelty, some fairy legend or ancient superstition; hither flocked the Danes in the ninth and tenth centuries, with their keen scent for battle and plunder, as to the richest district of Ireland;

F

here lived and sinned that princess Dearvorgil, famed in story, upon whom has been placed the responsibility of having occasioned the English invasion in 1169; here raged relentless warfare between the dwellers within the Pale and the fierce Irish chieftains; and here, in modern times, was fought and won the great pitched battle between Protestantism and the last of the Stewart kings on the soil of the United Kingdom.

In glancing at this celebrated valley, we shall pass in review some of its most attractive sites, and recall a few of its most famous associations. Reversing the natural order of the river, we will ascend from the estuary towards the source. A great river like the Boyne, draining a rich agri-cultural country, necessarily possesses a port of the first rank. Drogheda (pronounced Draw-edd-a) is to-day one of the busiest towns in Ireland, and for many past centuries the pulses of a strong and active life have throbbed here. It is well situated on the steep banks of the Boyne, having many features in common with an ordinary continental town, and, when seen from a distance, it arouses the expectations of the traveller; but a closer inspection tends to modify first impressions, and adds another to the manifold evidences of the truth of that trite saying, 'distance lends enchantment to the view.'

THE ST. LAWRENCE GATE, DROGHEDA.

From the earliest times Drogheda has figured more or less prominently in the history of Ireland. It was formerly a walled and strongly-fortified city, and although, unlike Derry, it has lost most of the ancient walls, some fine specimens yet remain. Chief among these is the St. Lawrence Gate, as perfect a specimen of that class of architecture as we could wish to see. As the wayfarer passes beneath the archway, and looks at the lofty towers, pierced by narrow windows and loopholes, imagination begins to picture the angry conflicts upon which it has looked down, and the successive generations that have passed in and out by its well-trodden entrance.

Drogheda stands by the site of an ancient ford. In process of time, as at Dublin and elsewhere, the fords were rendered needless by the con-struction of bridges. To the bridge built over the Boyne at this spot the town owes its name, *Droichead-atha*, the Bridge of the Ford, from which the present name Drogheda is easily derived. The name indicates also that this was the *first* bridge built over the Boyne on the northern coast road. The quays along the river, crowded as they are by steamers and vessels of many kinds, give proof that the town is not only an important place on the northern road, but that by the waterways of the ocean she is in communication with distant parts of the earth.

It is believed by some that Milesius and his followers landed near the town, that in the struggle with the natives, his son Coalpha perished, the fact being commemorated in the name, Coelph, given to one of the parishes. It is more certain that Patrick passed by the ford on his way to Slane; that early in the tenth century it became a stronghold from which the Danes ravaged the surrounding country; that in 1395 Richard II. held an assembly in the church of Mary Magdalene, and that there four Irish chieftains did homage and fealty to the English monarch. 'Every one of them, before the words of submission, laid aside his cap, belt and skeyne, and kneeling down before the king, put both his hands joined between the king's hands, and repeated the words of fealty and submission in the Latin language.' In Henry VII.'s reign a parliament was held at Drogheda, in 1494, under the Lord Deputy, Edward Poynings, which passed the

THE BRIDGE, DROGHEDA.

notorious 'Poynings Act,' by which it was decreed that the Irish Parliament should only deal with such matters as had already been approved by the Privy Council.

But the ever-memorable incident in Drogheda's history happened in 1649, when she attempted to withstand the greatest Englishman of the seventeenth century, who came to Ireland at the head of his veteran army, to bring the country back to the control of the British Parliament after its revolt and fearful massacres of the Protestants in 1641. Wide is the divergence of view as to what took place; not with regard to the facts—they are as clear as the sunlight—but as to the moral judgment to be passed upon them. In September, 1649, Oliver Cromwell summoned the garrison to surrender, 'To the which receiving no satisfactory answer,' his army stormed the town and put almost the whole garrison to the sword. Cromwell did not hesitate to give his view and justification of the deed.

F 2

' I am persuaded that this is a righteous judgment of God upon these barbarous wretches, who have imbued their hands with so much innocent blood ; and that it will tend to prevent the effusion of blood in the future. Which are the satisfactory grounds to such actions, which otherwise cannot but work remorse and regret.' ' Such,' writes Carlyle, ' was the storm of Drogheda. A thing which, if one *wanted* good assurance as to the essential meaning of it, might well " work remorse and regret": for indisputably the outer body of it is emphatic enough ! Cromwell, not in a light or loose manner, but in a very solemn and deep one, takes charge for himself at his own peril, that it *is* a judgment of God ; and that it *did* save " much effusion of blood " we and all spectators can very readily testify . . . . In fact, it cut through the heart of the Irish War. Wexford storm followed (not by forethought, it would seem, but by chance of war) in the same stern fashion ; and there was no other storm or slaughter needed in that country.'

The monuments of the past still existing in Drogheda are hardly so numerous as might be expected. There are the two ancient gate-towers, some traces of the old walls, the ruined church of St. Mary, and the fine tower of St. Mary Magdalene, the latter dating from the fourteenth century. Hence, most visitors prefer not to linger long in the town, and are eager to get out into the beautiful country, studded with sites and objects of interest, by which it is surrounded. Few excursions in Ireland can rival a day's wandering in the Boyne Valley, provided only that the sun be shining and the atmosphere clear enough to disclose the distant views.

Leaving the town in a jaunting car, and travelling by a road skirting the southern bank of the Boyne, whence fine views are obtained, Oldbridge is reached after a short drive. This name is now somewhat of a misnomer, as a comparatively new bridge spans the stream. But the interest of the scene, apart from its rural beauty, which is very great, centres in the event commemorated by the obelisk standing hard by the northern end of the bridge. Upon a huge irregular block of granite rises a massive column, erected in 1736, bearing this inscription : 'Sacred to the glorious memory of King William the Third, who, on the 1st of July, 1690, passed the river near this place to attack James the Second at the head of a Popish army, advantageously posted on the south side of it, and did, on that day, by a single battle, secure to us and to our posterity, our liberty, laws, and religion. In consequence of this action, James the Second left this kingdom and fled to France.'

On this eventful day William's army was posted along the north bank, and James's clustered around Donore Hill, on the south side of the river. Part of the English army crossed early in the morning by a ford a few miles up the river, thus outflanking the left wing of the Irish army and throwing it into some confusion. At this moment the remainder of

William's army crossed at Oldbridge, a severe struggle taking place, in which the Duke of Schomberg, Walker of Derry, and others were slain. James, it must be admitted, did nothing to encourage his army, and very early in the day fled to Dublin. Many of his troops fought bravely, but they were out-generalled, and were unable to stand before the trained valour of William's troops. The Irish army was routed and pursued some six miles beyond Duleek.

The site of this battle is interesting on many accounts, and the results of the victory were of the highest importance. But the associations of angry political passion, bloodshed and strife, seem strangely unsuitable to the peaceful scenes and lovely landscapes of the district; and so we gladly pursue our journey to places which speak to us of better things than war and bloodshed. From the northern end of the bridge a little dell runs up through the hill. It is well wooded and a carriage road passes through it. It is

THE BOYNE OBELISK.

known now as King William's Glen, because part of his army was posted here, and because he reached the river bank by this road on the day of his eventful crossing. The road leads up to the higher ground, and after a drive of from two to three miles, the ruins of Mellifont Abbey come into view. The drive is enjoyable, but not nearly so fine as many others in this neighbourhood. The car turns into a narrow valley, and after running a short distance, suddenly and without any indication of the nearness of

the ruins, brings the traveller to the peaceful shut-in *cul-de-sac* occupied by
Mellifont.

The first and most conspicuous object is a lofty, massive tower, through
whose arch, only a few years ago, a mill-race was carried, the water of
which supplied motive power to a mill which greatly disfigures the otherwise
picturesque cluster of ruins. But this, like so many mills all over Ireland,
has ceased to be profitable, is now closed, and the mill-race is dry. The
tower is 'square in shape and stern in aspect, and bears an elevated turret
at its north-eastern angle. This frowning portal, which still remains nearly
entire, and was evidently the chief entrance to the monastic enclosure, is
an historic evidence, fully as authentic, and more truth-telling than books,
of the state of the surrounding country at the time of its erection ; and
while the peaceful consecrated structures in the enclosure below are landmarks of learning and religion within, this bold castle tells a tale of
lawlessness and rapine which raged without. From this point we look down
upon a confused mass of ruins, arches, churches, solid blocks of ancient
masonry, some standing, others prostrate, several ivy-clad walls and grass-
grown mounds, a few dirty thatched cabins, with an ugly square-slated mill,
and an adjoining farm-yard.' [1]

This monastery, the first belonging to the Cistercian order of monks in
Ireland, was founded in 1142 by Malachy O'Morgair, Archbishop of Armagh,
and Donough O'Carroll, King of Oirgialla, *i.e.*, of the counties of Armagh,
Monaghan and Lough. The first company of monks were sent over from
his monastery at Clairvaulx by the famous St. Bernard, and by them the
first foundation was built. 'Then was the underwood cleared away, the oak
and the birch fell beneath the woodman's axe, and the wolf and the wild
boar were scared from their lurking-place, as the valley rang with the clang
of hammers and the sharp chip of the chisel. The bees, for which the
place was celebrated, and from which it was named, no longer gathered
their winter store from its sweet flowers ; and where the crane and the bittern
found their resting-place, arose the stately structures of the abbey and
surrounding monastic edifices, by far the most gorgeous which had yet been
seen in this country. There, where the cooing of the wild pigeon, or
the shrill whistle of the lapwing, alone were heard in former years, the
tolling of the vesper and the matin bell spread in measured cadences
over the surrounding woodlands, and the perfume of incense rose up
from the depths of the once solitary and uncultured valley of the
Matlock.' [2]

The first abbot was Christian O'Conarchy, appointed in 1145 ; here, in
1157, a famous synod was held, attended by seventeen bishops and Murtough
O'Loughlin, King of Ireland, who made rich presents to the abbey ; here,
in 1193, died the ill-fated Dearvorgil. It was bestowed upon Sir Gerald

---

[1] *The Boyne and the Blackwater*, p. 279.   [2] *Ibid.* p. 285.

Moore at the Dissolution of the Monasteries, and he changed it into a magnificent residence. Subsequently it was captured by the Irish in 1641.

The chief ruins within the enclosure are St. Bernard's Chapel and the Baptistery. The former when complete must have been a beautiful and highly ornate example of the Norman or Early English pointed style. The structure known as the Baptistery is unique, there being no other like it in Ireland. Originally it was an octagonal building, standing upon a series of splendidly built arches. In the opinion of good judges it dates from the early part of the twelfth century. Around these more important structures are the remains of pillars, crypts, arches, and all the evidences of the existence here in the past of a large church and extensive monastery. Sir W. Wilde has noted one important and significant fact connected with these ruins. 'One cannot fail to be struck with the remarkable fact that there is not a single characteristic emblem or element of true Irish ecclesiastical architecture at Mellifont; no round tower, no crosses, no inscriptions on tombs, no doorways with straight lintels and inclining jambs, and no knotted tracery, indicative of early Irish art. Everything we meet here is foreign.'[1]

RUINS OF THE BAPTISTERY, MELLIFONT.

True as this statement is with regard to Mellifont, it certainly does not apply to Monasterboice, only about three miles distant. No place in Ireland exhibits more magnificent specimens of distinctive Irish architecture. The car passes from Mellifont along the upland by a hilly road, and at length brings us to an enclosure situated on the slope of a gently-rising ground, from which towers aloft a bold but partly ruined Round Tower. The enclosure is a cemetery, and occupies the site of a religious house, founded here so far back as the sixth century by St. Buithe or Boetius. The Annals give A.D. 521 as the year of his death. The records of the foundation are tolerably complete, consisting mainly of the names and year of death of the abbots, and records of the plundering it endured. It was famous for learning and hospitality, and until Mellifont was founded ranked as the chief abbey of North-eastern Ireland.

The enclosure contains two ruined churches, the tower, three stone crosses, and some early tombstones. One of the churches, that nearest the

[1] *The Boyne and the Blackwater* p. 292.

tower, is the more ancient, dating in all probability from the ninth century; the other is a much later structure. The tower is a very fine example, being 50 feet in circumference at the bottom and about 90 feet high. It has been shattered at the top by lightning, and is somewhat out of the perpendicular. All who can spare the time should visit Monasterboice; those who are interested in Irish art, because there they can study *in situ* the most superb ancient crosses which Ireland can show; and those who feel no such interest, in order that, if possible, it may be developed, and thereby a new intellectual pleasure be enjoyed. The crosses are three in number. They are elaborately carved, and although the rains and sunshine, the haps and hazards of nine hundred years have passed since they were erected, many of the carvings upon them are still clear and sharp, and they enable the observer to form a clear idea of the devotion and skill concerned in their construction. Either time has dealt with them in kindlier fashion, or their material is more endurable; at any rate they are in better preservation than their great rivals at Clonmacnoise.

THE CROSS OF MUIREDACH, MONASTERBOICE.

These crosses are monumental, and upon one of them occurs the inscription 'A prayer for Muiredach, by whom was made this cross.' Now there were two abbots of Monasterboice who bore this name. One died in 844, the other in 923 or 924. The latter seems to have been a man of greater influence and power than the former, and this fact, coupled with other inferential evidence, has led archæologists to assign the cross to him. Hence it is at least over 950 years old. It has been found impossible to decipher satisfactorily the meaning of all the groups of sculpture. The marvel is that they have retained so well all these centuries their sharpness of outline. Miss Stokes' states, 'These six subjects—that is, the Crucifixion with its type, the Sacrifice of Isaac; the empty tomb guarded by sleeping soldiers, with the types of the Descent into Hell, Samson with Lion and Bear, David with Goliath; Christ in Glory—are the only ones that have been explained out of the twenty-four panels of this monument.'

Speaking of this cross, Mr. W. F. Wakeman, the well-known writer on Irish archæology, states,² 'Its height is exactly fifteen feet, and its breadth at the arm six. The figures of warriors and ecclesiastics and other sculpturings upon this cross retain in a remarkable degree their original sharpness of execution. The former are invaluable, affording as they do an excellent idea of the dress both military and ecclesiastical in use amongst the Irish during the ninth or tenth century. Most of the designs clearly refer to Scripture story. There are figures of warriors armed with swords, spears and other weapons, amongst which the axe and sling are conspicuous. The men, it may be observed, bear small circular targets like those in use to a late period among the Highlanders of Scotland.'

The cross immediately in front of the tower is more slender but much higher than Muiredach's. It is about 23 feet high, and consists of three stones, a shaft 11 feet long, the central stone containing the cross 6 feet 3 inches long, and the cap 2 feet 3 inches in height. It is 2 feet broad and 15 inches thick in the shaft. It has been badly chipped where the shaft is inserted into the base, but many of the sculptures are still fairly decipherable, among them being the Fall of Man, the Expulsion from Eden, the Worship of the Magi, and the Crucifixion. When and by whom it was erected is not known.

Of the third cross only a fragment remains, the burden of its destruction being placed upon Cromwell's broad shoulders.

The graveyard is still in use, and within the more ancient church is a circular granite stone, probably the shaft of an ancient font. Whenever a funeral takes place, the body is carried around the enclosure and then placed for a few minutes upon this stone. In the *Dublin Penny Journal* is a description of this scene, interesting for its own sake, and also because it came from the pen of Dr. Petrie, with which we close our sketch of Monasterboice—

'In its present deserted and ruined state it is a scene of the deepest and most solemn interest; and the mind must indeed be dull and earthly in which it fails to awaken feelings of touching and permanent interest. Silence and solitude the most profound are impressed on all its time-worn features. We are among the dead only, and we are forced, as it were, to converse with men of other days. In all our frequent visits to these ruins we never saw a living human being among them but once. It was

---

¹ *Early Christian Art in Ireland*, p. 135.   ² *Guide to Ireland*, p. 148.

during a terrific thunderstorm, which obliged us to seek shelter behind one of the stone crosses for an hour. The rain poured down in impetuous torrents, and the clouds were so black as to give day the appearance of night. It was at such an awful hour that a woman of middle age, finely formed, and of noble countenance, entered the cemetery, and regardless of the storm raging around, flung herself down upon a grave, and commenced singing an Irish lamentation in tones of heart-rending melancholy and surpassing beauty. This she carried on as long as we remained; and her voice, coming on the ear between the thunder peals, had an effect singularly wild and unearthly; it would be fruitless to attempt a description of it. The reader, if he knows what an Irishwoman's song of sorrow is, must imagine the effect it would have at such a moment among those lightning-shattered ruins, and chanted by such a living vocal monument of human woe and desolation. We subsequently learned, on inquiry, that this poor creature's history was a sad one; she was slightly crazed, in consequence of the death of her only son, who had been drowned; and her mania lay in a persuasion, which nothing could remove, that he was not lost, but would yet return to bless her, and close her long-weeping eyes in peace.'

At Oldbridge we are in the midst of modern events and associations, at Mellifont mediæval, and at Monasterboice in early historic. But the Boyne Valley has links with a far remoter past than the sixth century, the men of a much earlier generation have left us considerable traces of their handiwork. Between Oldbridge and Slane a large number of sepulchral mounds exist, and the references in the Irish MSS. enable scholars to decide that here is situated the great royal cemetery, used by the pagan kings of Ireland away back towards the beginning of the Christian era. Three enormous mounds, lying within a short distance of each other, are so much more prominent than their numerous smaller companions that they naturally for long years past have enjoyed the largest share of public attention. Visiting them as they lie upon the road to Slane, they come in the following order : Dowth, New Grange, and Knowth. To a superficial observer they appear natural hillocks ; but a cursory study suffices to convince one that they are the work of man. Indeed, it is, perhaps, not too much to say that they are, for their class, amongst the most wonderful works of man in the United Kingdom.

In the year 266 A.D. a famous Irish king named Cormac Mac Art died, 'the bone of a salmon sticking in his throat.' This event took place at the House of Cletty, supposed by some to be Clady on the Boyne. In a very ancient Irish treatise, the *History of the Cemeteries*, the following passage occurs : 'And he (Cormac) told his people not to bury him at Brugh, because it was a cemetery of idolaters ; for he did not worship the same God as any of those interred at Brugh ; but to bury him at Ros-na-Righ, with his face to the east. He afterwards died, and his servants of trust held a council, and came to the resolution of burying him at Brugh, the place where the Kings of Tara, his predecessors, were buried. The body of the king was thrice raised to be carried to Brugh, but the Boyne

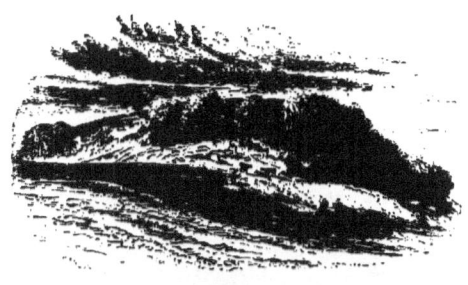

NEW GRANGE.

swelled up thrice, so as that they could not come ; so that they observed that it was violating the judgment of a prince to break through this testament of a king ; and they afterwards dug his grave at Ros-na-Righ, as he himself had ordered.' The same record also states, 'The nobles of the Tuatha De Danaan were used to bury at Brugh.' On the banks of the river two miles below Slane is a place called, to this day, Rosnaree, evidently the ford referred to in the old MS., and the great mounds on the other bank are doubtless the cemetery Brugh, in which Cormac, having become a Christian, did not wish to sleep with his pagan ancestors.

Dowth was opened and examined in 1847, and it was soon made manifest that it was a great tomb ; but nothing was unearthed or discovered superior to what had been accessible for many years in the mound of New Grange, a mile or two nearer Slane. This consists of an enormous cairn of stones upwards of 70 feet high, covering from one to two acres, and weighing, it

STANDING STONES AT NEW GRANGE.

has been computed, 180,000 tons. Once it was surrounded by a circle of huge stones, but only ten of these remain. At intervals excavations for road making or building purposes have been made in its sides, reducing its bulk. It is not known when or by whom the entrance was first discovered and explored, but as early as 1699 a description of it was written, which agrees in all essential particulars with what any visitor can now see. The entrance is by a low passage, which starts from an enormous stone, 10 feet long, 18 inches thick, and finely carved with a bold spiral pattern. The passage runs nearly north and south, and is 63 feet long. It is constructed of upright stones, twenty-one on the right and twenty-two on the left side, covered in by great flag-stones, one of these measuring no less than *seventeen feet by six*. One can creep along the greater part of this passage with ease, but about 20 feet from the inner chamber the side stones have either fallen or been pressed in so as to nearly touch at the top. Here the explorer has nothing for it but to go down on hands and knees and crawl. The guide with the light who goes before proves that it can be done, and few are likely to experience any difficulty. None should allow this small drawback to prevent them from seeing a marvellous piece of work, viz:—the great sepulchral chamber, occupying the whole centre of the mound.

After squeezing through the narrow but colossal portal the way becomes easier, and we pass into a lofty domed chamber. The dim light—when we saw it a fairly strong paraffin lamp was used—the strange entrance, the outlines, at first so shadowy and awe-inspiring, all combine to make such a visit memorable. As the eye gets used to the chamber it is seen to consist of a central apartment with three recesses, one opposite the entrance, one to the east and one to the west.

ENTRANCE TO NEW GRANGE.

One of these is depicted in our engraving. It is 9 feet high, 8 deep and 7 wide. The central chamber is formed by eleven stones, with flat surfaces facing inwards. From these as a base course, rises the dome, formed of large stones placed horizontally, each layer projecting a little beyond that directly beneath it, thus forming a structure of the 'bee-hive' type, closed and clamped at the top by an enormous slab of rock. This chamber has a diameter of 18 feet and a height of 19 feet 6 inches.

Such is the sepulchral mound of New Grange. It is impossible to stand in that weird chamber without having the brain and the imagination excited. When were these massive stones piled up with such rude and yet, for their purpose, effective skill? How did these men of a pre-Christian age acquire mechanical power sufficient to lift such masses as the roofing slab of the entrance or the keystone of the dome? What manner of men were they who could create such lordly dwellings for their dead? What ideas of life and death and the future did these mighty builders have? One would like to get the clue to these and to many such questions. But at present the answers are vague and uncertain. Not yet, with all our increased research and knowledge, have we explained the mystery. New Grange drives home upon the thoughtful observer the lesson conveyed by the old saying, 'There were kings before Agamemnon.' There were men in Ireland before historians arose to chronicle their deeds; there were conceptions of man's work and power and pride that produced these august tombs. May we not say that there is evidence here that the pre-historic man had a brain to conceive, an arm to execute, and a heart to feel, for the time in which he lived, quite equal to those of his remote nineteenth-century brother, who is apt sometimes to talk and to reason as if knowledge began with him, and as if the men of the early ages were nothing but children?

A pleasant drive of a couple of miles takes us past Knowth, the third of these great mounds, as yet, so far as is known, unexplored. A steep descent brings us to the little town of Slane. And here indeed we are on classic ground. A somewhat long ascent, but one easily made by car, brings us to the Hill of Slane.

Upon this hill, on Easter Eve, St. Patrick kindled his paschal fire, according to the habit of that day. This was contrary to the custom, that at the annual festival held at that time of the year at Tara, no fire should be lit in the neigh-

RECESS IN THE SEPULCHRAL CHAMBER, NEW GRANGE.

bourhood until the great fire had been kindled at the palace of Tara. Thus began the series of events that led to St. Patrick's intercourse with King Laoghaire. And, however it may be with this story, and certain as it is that later miracle-makers have woven about the history of Patrick a web of absurd wonder-workings, it nevertheless remains a fact that this district is inseparably connected with the life and work of the great teacher, and that this connection rests upon a sure basis of fact. The faith and zeal of after ages crowned the hill with a monastery and a cathedral. The tower still stands, albeit in a ruinous condition; and it can be ascended by the adventurous. From its summit a superb view—unsurpassable in its kind in Europe—is obtained. Seen under such circumstances as those which favoured the writer, viz. brilliant May sunshine, and a clear atmosphere and an early summer stillness, the truth of the following description is evident :

'The ground whereon we stand is sacred, consecrated by the footprints of our patron saint, hallowed by the dust of kings. Look abroad over the wide undulating plains of Meath, or to the green hills of Louth : where in the broad landscapes of Britain, find we a scene more fruitful and varied, or one more full of interesting heart-stirring associations ? Climb this tower and cast your eye along the river. Look from the tall, pillar-like form of the yellow steeple at Trim, which rises in the distance, to where yon bright line marks the meeting of the sea and sky below the Maiden Tower at Drogheda, and trace the clear blue waters of the Boyne winding through this lovely, highly cultivated landscape, so rich in all that can charm the eye and awaken the imagination ; take into view the hills of Skreen and Tara ; pass in review the woods of Hayes, Ardmulchan, Beauparc ; look down into the green mounds and broad pastures of Slane ; follow the Boyne below you, as it dances by each ford and rapid, to where the great pyramids of Western Europe, Knowth, New Grange and Dowth, rise on its left bank ; see you not the groves of Townley Hall and Old Bridge, marking the battle-field of 1690 with the ill-fated hill of Donore, where the sceptre passed for ever from the line of Stuart, obtruding its long-remembered tale of civil strife upon us ? Duleek stands in the distance. Beyond those hills that border Louth lie Monasterboice and Mellifont, the last resting-place of the faithless Bride of Brefney.

'Those steeples and turrets which rise in the lower distance were shattered by the balls of Cromwell ; and that knoll which juts above them is the Mill Mount of Drogheda. What a picture have we here from this Richmond Hill of Irish scenery ! What an extensive page of our country's history does it unfold to us ! What recollections gush upon us as we stand on the abbey walls of Slane, and take in this noble prospect at a glance ! The records and footprints of two thousand years are all before us ; the solemn procession of the simple shepherd to the early pagan mound, the rude slinger standing on the earthen circle, the Druid fires paling before the bright sun of Christianity, the cadence of the round tower's bell, the matin and the vesper hymn swelling from the hermit's cell or early missionary church ; the proud galleys and glancing swords of fierce Northern hordes ; the smoking ruins of church and tower, the shout of rival clans in civil feuds ; the lances and banners of Norman soldiers ; the moat and fosse and drawbridge of the keep, still echoing back the strife of hostile ranks, the native for his soil, the stranger for his hire ; the ford defended and the castle won ; the pilgrim's cross, the stately abbey, and the baron's hall ; in church, the stole ejected for the surplice, the town besieged, the city sacked ; and then the rattle, and the roar, and smoke of recent battle—have one and all their epochs, ruins, sites, or history, legibly inscribed upon this picture.'[1]

Where better than in connection with these scenes once visited by Patrick can we say what is needful concerning his life and influence? All who are in even a small measure acquainted with the facts know that controversy has raged in the past over almost every statement connected with Patrick's life. In fact, some have gone so far as to deny his existence altogether. The ablest and most comprehensive work on the subject which has appeared in recent years is the edition of the Tripartite Life of St. Patrick, taken from the Book of Armagh, and edited by Dr. Whitley Stokes. In the introduction to this work he gives the following admirable summary of what is known, and what is probable. Considerable differences of opinion with regard to certain points may be permitted. For example, many will hesitate to believe that Patrick spent thirty years of unsuccessful ministry in Ireland, and then, attributing this failure to want of episcopal ordination and Roman authority, went to Gaul to get these! Yet the compendium of the personal history is so clear and so reasonably put that it gives a complete picture of the saint's long life. We venture to quote Dr. Stokes' words:

'All the facts that can be stated with certainty about St. Patrick are these :—He was born in the latter half of the fourth century, and was reared a Christian. He had relations (*parentes*) in the Britains, and he calls these Britains his *patria*. His father Calpornus, or rather Calpornius, son of Potitus, was both a deacon and a decurio, and therefore belonged to a Roman Colony. Potitus was son of a deacon named Odissus. Patrick's father lived at a place called Bannavem Taberniae, near which he had a small farm, and there, in his sixteenth year, Patrick was taken captive. His captors took him to Ireland, with several others. There he was employed in herding sheep or swine, and devoted himself greatly to prayer. When he had remained six years with his master he ran away, and embarked at some place about two hundred miles distant. After a three days' voyage he landed, and for twenty-eight days journeyed through a desert to his home.

'Again, after a few years, but while he was still a young man (*puer*), he was in the Britians with his parents, when he dreamed that he was summoned to Ireland, and awoke much pricked in heart.

'He gave up home and parents and *ingenuitas* (that is, the status of a free man born free), to preach the Gospel to the Irish tribes. His motives, he says, were the Gospel and its promises, and Secundinus adds, that he received his apostleship from God, and was sent by God as an apostle, even as Paul. He travelled through the Gauls and Italy, and spent some time in the islands in the Tyrrhene Sea. One of these appears to have been Lerina, or St. Honorat. He had been ordained a deacon, probably a priest, and at some time in his career a bishop.

---

[1] *The Boyne and the Blackwater*, pp. 179, 180.

'Long after the dream above mentioned, and when he was almost worn out (*prope deficiebam*), he returned to Ireland (whether for the first or second time will be afterwards considered), and travelling through the remotest parts of the country, he made known the faith to the Irish tribes, of whom he baptized many thousand men. The Lord's flock, he says, was increasing rapidly, and he could not count the sons of the Scots and the knights' daughters who were becoming monks and virgins of Christ. He also ordained clergy, and taught at least one priest from his infancy. His success excited the jealousy of the rhetoricians of the Gauls, in which country he had brethren (*fratres*).'[1]

'He was well versed in the Latin Scriptures, both canonical and apocryphal, and though he speaks contemptuously of his own learning, his Latin is not much more rustic than that of Gregory of Tours. He appears to have known little or no Greek. Irish, of course, he learned during his six years of bondage.

'He was modest, shrewd, generous, enthusiastic, with the Celtic tendency to exaggerate failure and success. Like St. Paul, he was desirous of martyrdom. He was physically brave, and had strong passions, which he learned to control. He speaks of twelve *pericula* in which his *anima* was ventured, beside many snares (ambuscades ?) and things which he was unable *verbis exprimere.*

'This is all that can be stated with certainty about Patrick, his life, writings, creed, learning and character. When and where he was born, his mother's name, his baptismal name, where he was captured, when and by whom he was educated, when and by whom he was ordained, when he returned to Ireland; whether he afterwards left that country, whether he travelled as a missionary, the date of his death, the place of his burial; on each of these points we have only the statements, sometimes discrepant and sometimes obviously false, contained in the later lives of St. Patrick and other late documents.'[2]

'Of these statements the following are the least improbable—

'Patrick was born about the year 373, at Nemptor, an old Celtic *Neme-toduron*, which may have been the older name for *Ail Cluade* (Rock of Clyde), now Dumbarton.

'The place where Patrick was captured (about A.D. 390), Bannavem Taberniae, has not been identified, but was probably somewhere on the western sea coast (*armorica*) of North Britain. His captor took him to the north-east of Ireland, and sold him to a chief named Miliuc, who named him Cothraige, and employed him in herding swine in the valley of the Braid near Slemmish. After six years—when he was therefore in his twenty-third year—he escaped and returned to his family in Britain. As to what he did during the next thirty-seven years, *i.e.,* from A.D. 396

[1] *The Tripartite Life of St. Patrick,* vol. i., pp. cxxxiii. cxxxiv.   *Ibid.* pp. cxxxv. cxxxvi.

to 432, it is impossible to offer anything but conjectures more or less plausible.

'The current tradition is that after a second captivity, which lasted only two months, he betook himself to the best schools of the West of Europe, and first came to Ireland to preach the Gospel in the sixtieth year of his age. But against this four objections may be urged. First, if Patrick had been absent from Ireland in Gaulish schools from the age of twenty-three to the age of sixty, he would certainly have forgotten Irish, which language he seems to have known well on returning to that country. Secondly, he would have learned to write better Latin than that of his *Confession* and the *Letter to Coroticus*, and he would not have complained by implication that he had not been *in sermonibus instructus et eruditus*. Thirdly, it is improbable that an ardent nature like his, spurred by visions and eager to annex a new territory to the kingdom of Christ, would have postponed his attempt for thirty-seven years. And, fourthly, this alleged long absence from Ireland is plainly inconsistent with Patrick's own words, "Ye know and God knows how I have lived among you from my youth up, both faithful in truth and sincere in heart."'

'It therefore seems probable that Patrick, after his escape from his second captivity, studied in Gaul until he was fit for ordination as a priest. That he was ordained by a Gaulish bishop, and that he then, moved, it may be, by one of the visions which he had so often, returned to Ireland and commenced his work as a missionary.'

'The kernel of fact in the story told by Probus about his ordination seems to be that Patrick returned to Ireland on or soon after his ordination as priest (say in A.D. 397), and without any commission from Rome; that he laboured for thirty years in converting the pagan Irish, but met with little or no success; that he attributed this failure to the want of episcopal ordination and Roman authority; that in order to have these defects supplied he went back to Gaul (say in A.D. 427), intending ultimately to proceed to Rome; that he spent some time in study with Germanus of Auxerre; that hearing of the failure and death of Palladius, who had been sent on a mission to Ireland by Pope Celestinus, in A.D. 431, he was directed by Germanus to take at once the place of the deceased missionary; that Patrick thereupon relinquished his journey to Rome, received episcopal consecration from a Gaulish bishop, Matorix, and returned a second time to Ireland about the year 432, when he was sixty years old, as a missionary from the Gaulish Church, and supplied with Gaulish assistants and funds for his mission. In this there is no improbability, no necessity to alter dates to assume a plurality of Patricks, a duality of Paladii, and so transfer the acts of one to another.

'There is nothing improbable in the tradition that Patrick landed at the

---

[1] *The Tripartite Life of St. Patrick*, vol. i., pp. cxxxvii. cxxxviii.

G

mouth of the River Vartry, where the town of Wicklow now stands, and where about a year before Palladius had landed. Thence Patrick sailed northward along the coast, touching at Inis Patrick, stopping at the mouth of the Boyne and landing at Strangford Lough. There he converted the chieftain Dichu, and received from him the site of the church called Sabhall Patraic, a name still in existence as Saul. Thence Patrick went to the valley of his captivity, to visit his old master Miliuc, and offer him a double ransom ; and there occurred the event which is commonly called a legend, but which seems to be an instance either of *dharna*[1] or of propitiatory self-sacrifice. Miliuc, seeking to prevent the triumphant approach of his former slave, burnt himself along with his substance and his house.

'Patrick then returned to Dichu's residence in Maghinis, and there he remained many days, and the faith began to grow in that place.

'After leaving Dichu he sailed to the mouth of the Boyne, and leaving his boats proceeded on foot to Slane, where he lighted his paschal fire, and the next day went on to Tara, chanting the hymn called *The Deer's Cry.* There he preached Christ before the Irish over-king Loiquire, and converted his chief bard, Dubthach Maccu-Lugair.

'From Tara Patrick went to Telltown, where Cabre, the king's brother, sought to slay him, and caused his attendants to be scourged into the River Blackwater. Conall Gultan, however, the king's youngest brother, received Patrick hospitably, and gave him the site of a church. Patrick then proceeded actively in the conversion of Bregia and other parts of the territory of the Southern Hui Néill. He then travelled to Tirawley under a safe-conduct from the nobles of that country, for which he seems to have paid in gold and silver "the price of fifteen souls of men"; and in Tirawley, near the present town of Killala, he converted the local king and a great multitude of his subjects.

'After spending some years in Connaught, Patrick revisited Ulster, where he erected many churches, especially in Tirconnell. He then visited Meath, passed on to Leinster, and baptized at Naas the two sons of the king of that province. He next visited Magh-life, and entering Seix, now Queen's County, again met the converted bard Dubthach Maccu-Lugair, and made Dubthach's disciple, Frace, Bishop of Sletty. Thence he proceeded to Ossory, and thence to Munster, where he baptized the king.

'According to the *Tripartite Life,* St. Patrick then founded Armagh, the site of which he obtained from a chieftain named Dáire. After having spent sixty years in missionary work, partly as priest, partly as bishop, he died at an advanced age (perhaps ninety years), on the 17th March, probably in or about the year 463, and was buried in Downpatrick.

---

[1] A Hindi word meaning primarily the act of sitting in restraint at the door of a debtor by a creditor or his agent to enforce payment. Then it came to mean fasting at a Temple door to extort favours from the idol, and later to indicate the Brahmanic practice of voluntarily sitting down to die by hunger.

'These are all, or almost all, the facts relating to Patrick which are either certain or reasonably probable. He seems, as Dr. Todd says, to have always addressed himself in the first instance to kings or chieftains, the baptism of the chieftain being immediately followed by the outward adherence of the clan; but it is certain that the whole of Ireland did not submit to Patrick's influence.

ROUND TOWER OF DONAGHMORE.

'Even when he wrote his *Confession* he tells us that he looked daily for a violent death (*internecio*), or to be brought back to slavery (*redigi in servitutem*), and there is some evidence that a partial apostacy took place during the two centuries following his death.'[1]

The many noted towns and districts in the upper valley of the Boyne

[1] *The Tripartite Life of St. Patrick*, vol. i., pp. cxli.-cxliii.

must be passed over with scant reference. They include Donaghmore, with the fine round tower so prominent in the great controversy upon the origin and use of these buildings, from the fact that above the doorway is a sculpture of the crucifixion. This was supposed by some to indicate that a pagan building had been thus consecrated to Christian use. Dr. Petrie holds that it rather fixes the date of the tower to be about the tenth century.

Navan, Kells, Bective Abbey, Trim, and Tara, are all well worth the attention of the leisured traveller. They are all rich in remains which indicate the part they have played in past history. At Tara, whose old Irish name, *Teamhair*, means an elevated spot commanding an extensive prospect, there is not only a view similar to but less comprehensive than that at Slane, but there are also evidences of the power of the early Irish kings. The spot ceased to be a royal residence as early as 563 A.D., and it is hardly needful to state that the evidences of past grandeur are not so conspicuous as at Cashel and Trim. The remains are chiefly *raths* or *duns*, that is, old mounds and enclosing fortifications of earth, that have evidently been residences in the past. The largest of these, Rath Riogh or Riga, is an oval 850 feet long, enclosing the mounds known as the Forradh and the Teach Cormaic, or House of Cormac. The Forradh is flat at the top and encircled by a double earth-work, enclosing a ditch. Upon the centre of this stands a stone pillar, placed there in 1798 to mark the graves of some who fell in conflict with the English troops. This pillar had lain for ages upon a neighbouring mound. Dr. Petrie held that it was the famed Lia Fail, or Stone of Destiny, upon which for many ages the Irish kings were crowned. This opinion is not shared by all scholars; if it be true, then this Lia Fail should be under the Coronation Chair in Westminster Abbey, in the place of the stone so long preserved there. To the north of the Forradh lie the remains of the great banqueting hall. These consist of two parallel lines of earth divided by openings, six on each side, which show where the ancient entrances stood; it was 360 feet long, and 40 wide. From the centre of the Forradh the finest view of the surrounding country is obtained.

Kells is a lively little town, situated near the Blackwater, celebrated as having been the residence of Columba, who founded a monastery there in 550, and as containing a round tower, a building known as St. Columbkille's house, and several splendid old Irish crosses. The saint's house belongs to the class of building and to the same age as St. Kevin's Kitchen, already described. One of the crosses is in the town, three are in the churchyard, and one, the finest of all, in the market place. Kells was in very remote times the home of learning and literature. The most conspicuous evidence of this is the Book of Kells, so fully described in Chapter I., which in all probability was written in the monastery in this town.

Trim, the last place in this rich valley we shall note, though of great antiquity, presents important remains only of much later date than its neighbours. Sir W. Wilde grows enthusiastic over its charms. 'To see Trim aright the tourist must approach it by the Blackbull Road from Dublin, when all the glorious ruins which crowd this historic locality, and which extend over a space of above a mile, burst suddenly upon him: the remains of St. John's Friary, and castellated buildings at Newtown; the stately abbey of St. Peter and St. Paul, a little farther on; the grey massive towers of King John's Castle; the Sheep Gate, and portions of the town wall; and, towering above all, the tall, commanding form of the Yellow Steeple, which seems the guardian genius of the surrounding ruins. All these beauteous objects, with the ancient church tower, the town itself, the Wellington Testimonial, and the modern public buildings, form a combination of scenery and an architectural diorama such as we have rarely witnessed.'[1]

The Yellow Steeple, a square tower, of which only the east and part of the north and south walls are standing, is 125 feet high, and was probably a watch tower. Immediately beside it, in ancient days, were the buildings of St. Mary's Abbey. The castle of King John, so called simply because that monarch once lodged in or near it, was built early in the thirteenth century, and has the proud pre-eminence of being the finest ruined castle in a country peculiarly rich in that class of architectural treasure. The ruins cover two acres; the donjon or keep rises to a height of eighty feet, and the walls in places are twelve feet thick. The castle was surrounded by a moat, 486 yards long, into which the waters of the Boyne could be admitted.

Here, during the last seven centuries, many a pageant has taken place, and many a tragedy been enacted. Men famous in history have stayed within these walls. 'We cannot forget the pageants and tournaments of Richard, Earl of Ulster, the imprisonment of the families of the Dukes of Gloucester and Lancaster, during Richard II.'s sojourn in this country; the confinement here of the royal hero of Agincourt; its occupation by the De Lacys, the Mortimers, the Verdons, the Cootes, its parliaments and its sieges—all of which throw a degree of splendour over the ruins of Trim.'[2]

In the early part of the fifteenth century, Sir John Talbot, 'the Scourge of France,' erected a castle at Trim, of which scarcely any traces remain.

Dangan, where the Duke of Wellington lived as a boy, is only five miles away, and on his twenty-first birthday Trim elected him as its representative in the Irish Parliament. Only two miles distant is Laracor, once the residence of Dean Swift; and along the quiet roads of this peaceful region he and Stella often sauntered.

[1] *The Boyne and the Blackwater*, p. 79.   [2] *Ibid.* p. 95.

ST. BRIGID'S CHURCH AND THE ROUND TOWER, KILDARE.
(From a photograph by Lawrence, of Dublin.)

CHAPTER IV.

FROM DUBLIN TO CORK.

THE trip from Dublin to Bantry is made by the main line of the Great Southern and Western Railway as far as Cork, and by this route some very beautiful country and some famous places are seen. Kilkenny and Cashel, Kilcolman and Youghal, Cork and Queenstown, the Golden Vale and Bantry Bay all lie either in our path or can be seen with a very slight expenditure of time and trouble.

The first stopping-place of the fast express is at Kildare, the Church of the Oak, the place where, under the shelter of an oak many centuries ago, St. Brigid built her cell. She was born near Dundalk, about 450 A.D., and founded in 484 a great religious house at Kildare, consisting of both monks and nuns. It is said that from the sixth to the thirteenth centuries, a fire, lighted by Brigid, was kept burning. The site of the cell in which it burned is still pointed out. She died about 525. For ages past a cathedral, dedicated to her, has stood on an elevated site in the town. On the dissolution of the religious houses it fell into a ruined condition, but in recent years attempts have been made to restore, or rather to rebuild it. The tower has been rebuilt and the nave is roofed in. The choir is now used as a parish church; but although much has been done to the nave and tower, they are yet very far from completion. Close by the church stands the round tower. It has been restored at the top, but unfortunately a turreted parapet has been substituted for the correct conical roof. The tower is in good preservation, is 130 feet high, and has a doorway which exhibits unusual features of interest. It is about fifteen feet from the ground, and consists of three concentric arches, ornamented with fine zig-zag mouldings. From the churchyard a fine view to the north and west is obtained, a conspicuous feature being the Chair of Kildare, a limestone mass on the hill called Grange.

Kildare is a junction for Carlow, Kilkenny and Waterford. The old town of Kilkenny is well worth a visit, because of its fine situation on

> The stubborn Newre, whose waters gray,
> By faire Kilkenny and Rosseponte boord,

because of the part it has played in Irish history, and because of the architectural treasures it yet possesses.

Well situated on an elevation overlooking the Nore, stands the castle which was originally built by William, Earl of Pembroke, 1195. It was purchased by James Butler, third Earl of Ormonde. In 1399 Richard II. was entertained here, and in March, 1650, Cromwell captured it. Within very recent years it has been thoroughly restored, although for centuries very little of the original building has been in existence.

Kilkenny in its name commemorates one of the early Christian teachers. The name means the Church of Cainnech or Canice, who was born in 517, and died in 600. He was also venerated

THE DOORWAY IN THE ROUND TOWER AT KILDARE.

in Scotland, under the name of Kenneth, and several churches in Argyleshire are named after him. The Cathedral of St. Canice is one of the best in Ireland, and, though named after the saint, is of course of a much later date. It was begun about 1180, and completed in the course of the next century. It is 226 feet long and 123 feet wide at the transepts. From the juncture of the nave and transepts a low but massive tower rises. The cathedral has a very fine western door; it contains many tombs, especially those of members of the Ormonde family. Near the south transept rises a round tower, perfect, with the exception of the conical roof.

Several Parliaments met here, the most notorious being that which passed in 1367 what were known as the Kilkenny Statutes, one of which enacted

that marriage with
the ' mere Irish '
was treason, and
that any one using
the Irish dress or
language should
forfeit his lands !

Leaving Kil-
dare and Kilkenny
behind, and hasten-
ing on towards the
west, the Rock of
Cashel next de-
serves attention.
Like Kilkenny,
only in much higher
degree, Cashel
combines beauty
of situation with a
wealth of ancient architectural remains and historical
associations. Cashel is a small country
town, not specially noteworthy in itself,
the houses of which cluster near the base
of a mass of limestone rock 300 feet
high. This mass of limestone forms the
far-famed Rock of Cashel. Rising as it
does very abruptly from the broad fertile
Golden Vale of Tipperary, it formed a
natural fortress, certain to be adapted
in warlike times to purposes of defence.
Equally certain also was it to become
the site of religious buildings. The
combination of castle and abbey, of
religious and military power, so frequently met with in Ireland, existed
here in full force. The ecclesiastical
remains are now much more prominent
than the military. Comparatively few
traces of the ancient fortifications remain,
but the eye is almost bewildered by
the towers and turrets and arches of
the churches ; yet the balance is well

ST. CANICE'S STEPS, KILKENNY.

THE ROCK OF CASHEL.

preserved. The mere appearance of the rock conveys a sense of strength and security, testifying to its ancient power; while there is a fitness, if choice must be made, in the fact that the splendid architectural remains tend to direct the thoughts of the observer from earthly might and splendour towards the kingdom of Heaven and the Prince of Peace.

The name reflects the past history of the country, for there were many Cashels scattered over Ireland in ancient days, and the word has long formed part of many proper names. It comes from the Irish *caiseal*, and signifies a circular stone fort. The rock at this particular Cashel having been in early times the stronghold of the kings of Munster, and having pre-eminent natural advantages, has in the course of time appropriated the generic as its own specific name.

The earliest historical references to Cashel describe it as the regal fortress of the kings of Munster. St. Patrick, according to the life in the Book of Armagh, visited Cashel, and converted the king. 'After this Patrick went into the province of Munster, to Cashel of the Kings. When Oengus, son of Natfraich, arose in the morning, all the idols were on their faces ; and Patrick, with his household, found him beside the fort. He gave them welcome and brought them into the fort to the place where Patrick's flagstone is to-day. And after this Patrick baptized Natfraich's sons, and left blessing and prosperity upon them ; and blessed the fort, namely Cashel, and said that until Doom only one slaughter should take place there. And he abode seven years in Munster.

'While Patrick was baptizing Oengus, the spike of the crozier went through Oengus's foot. Said Patrick, "Why didst thou not tell this to me ?" "It seemed to me," saith Oengus, "that it was a rite of the faith." "Thou shalt have its reward," said Patrick : "thy successor," that is, the seed of Oengus and Ailill, son of Natfraich, "shall not die of a wound from to-day for ever." No one is King of Cashel until Patrick instals him, and confers ecclesiastical rank upon him ; and twenty-seven kings of the race of Ailill and Oengus ruled in Cashel under a crosier until the time of Cenn-gecan (slain A.D. 897).'[1]

In 1101, according to the Annals of the Four Masters, a convocation of the people of the southern half of Ireland was held at Cashel, at which Murtough O'Brien, the king, gave Cashel to the devout, 'for the use of the religious in Ireland in general.' Murtough's successor, Cormac, built the famous chapel in 1134. In 1152 Cashel became the seat of the archbishopric of Munster, and soon after a cathedral was built. Henry II. here received the homage of Donnell O'Brien, King of Munster ; Edward Bruce held a parliament here ; in 1495 Gerald, Earl of Kildare, burnt the cathedral, *because* he thought the archbishop was inside. He was grieved afterwards to learn that his supposition was incorrect.

The chief buildings upon the Rock of Cashel are the round tower, Cormac's Chapel, and the ruined cathedral. The cluster of towers, arches and walls presents a most effective appearance as the traveller approaches the rock on his jaunting car. The round tower stands at the north-east corner of the north transept of the cathedral, is 90 feet high, 50 feet in circumference, and has walls 4 feet thick. It was divided into five stories or floors, and the masonry is said to be as good as that of the White Tower in the Tower of London. The original conical roof is still upon it. Although not specially mentioned in any of the Irish annals, there can be but little

---

[1] *Tripartite Life of St. Patrick*, vol. i., pp. 195, 197.

doubt that this is the most ancient of all the buildings now standing upon the rock.

Next in order of time, but supreme in historical and architectural interest, comes the unique Chapel of Cormac. This was begun by Cormac MacCarthy, King of Munster, in 1127, and consecrated in 1134 A.D. The entry in the Annals of Inisfallen runs : ' 1134. The church built by Cormac MacCarthy at Cashel was consecrated by the archbishop and bishops of Munster, at which ceremony the nobility of Ireland, both clergy and laity, were present.' Notwithstanding its great age, the edifice is in very good preservation, and presents many features of special interest to the student of ecclesiastical architecture. It differs in several respects from the common type. It has no east window in the chancel, and no original west door; it

THE INTERIOR OF CORMAC'S CHAPEL, CASHEL.

has both a north and south entrance, and at each side of the end of the nave a tower rises, the southern to a height of 55 feet, the northern 50. In the southern tower is a staircase leading to some crofts or apartments situated between the interior stone roof, and the high external vaulted roof; the chancel arch, which is very handsome, and is not placed in the centre, but at the southern side of the dividing wall. The arch is decorated with numerous carved human heads. The whole building is 50 feet long by 18 wide.

The north door, of which we give an engraving, is very richly decorated. It doubtless formed the original main entrance to the chapel. It consists of five concentric arches or mouldings, supported by five columns

and a double column. In the archway of the door is a sculpture repre-
senting a centaur shooting at a lion, which is tearing some other animal
beneath its paws.

A recess in the north wall holds a tomb said to be that of Cormac

NORTH DOORWAY, CORMAC'S CHAPEL, CASHEL.

MacCarthy; but there is reason to believe that it is later in date, Cormac's
tomb having been removed a century or so ago to the north transept of
the cathedral close by. The ornamentation on this latter tomb is twelfth
century work, and when it was opened many years ago a fine crozier was
found in it. This ultimately passed into Dr. Petrie's possession, who after

carefully studying the old annals came to the conclusion that Cormac was a bishop as well as a king, and hence that the crozier may be the one used by Cormac himself. The head only has survived, the rest being of perishable material. 'This is formed of copper, and measures 12 inches in length and 5 in the diameter of the crook. Its surface is covered with a sunk lozenge carving, filled with a vitreous enamel of a blue colour, the intervening elevations of which are gilt—a design obviously intended to represent the scales of a reptile. Within the curve is a human figure, standing, with one leg placed on the neck of the serpent, and the other on the back of a double-faced, wingless dragon, which he has pierced in the back with a spear which the dragon bites. This human figure is dressed in a simple tunic, tied round the waist; and the feet are covered with buskins which extend above the ankles. The bowl is encircled by a central belt ornamented with nine turquoises and nine sapphires, placed alternately and at equal distances from each other. Immediately above the bowl is an ornament resembling the Irish crown. The lower part or socket is ornamented with a very graceful pattern composed of leaves or flowers in three vertical ranges, separated from each other by three figures of a fish ; the well-known mystical symbol of the early Christians ; and these are each ornamented with a range of seven gems, turquoises and sapphires placed alternately at equal distances along the back.' [1]

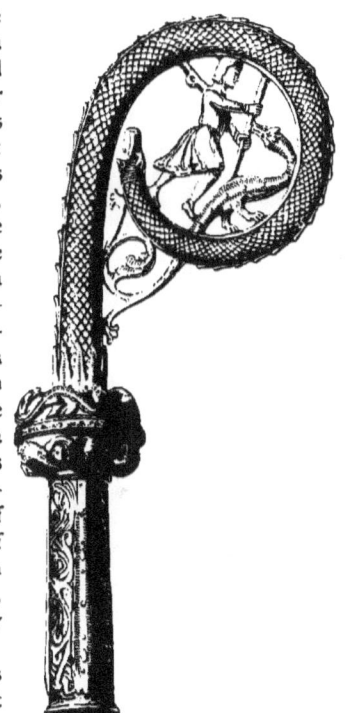

CROZIER FOUND ON OPENING A TOMB IN CORMAC'S CHAPEL, CASHEL.

In the cemetery adjoining the buildings there are no ancient crosses like those at Monasterboice ; but near the entrance to the cathedral stands what is known as the 'Cross of Cashel.' This when complete must have been a very fine piece of work. It is now greatly dilapidated, but enough of its ornamentation can be made out to prove that it most probably dates from the twelfth century. The figure cut in the stone is supposed to be St. Patrick, and the Kings of Munster are said to have been crowned while standing on its pedestal.

[1] *Round Towers of Ireland*, p. 313.

As already noted, the cathedral dates from the latter half of the twelfth century, but most of the work now standing was built about the close of the fourteenth. It is 260 feet long and 170 feet wide at the transept, and a large part of the fine central tower is still standing. It may be easily ascended, and from the top one of the best views in the south of Ireland is to be obtained. It was intact and used for Divine worship until the time of Archbishop Price, 1744–1752, who, according to tradition, not being able to drive his carriage up to the church-door, obtained an Act of Parliament to remove the cathedral to the town, and unroofed the old building for the sake of its lead! All subsequent attempts to restore it failed, and it now remains a melancholy but a picturesque ruin.

The Rock of Cashel affords material for a whole volume of antiquarian disquisition. Few places better reward the time spent in acquiring a fair knowledge of the remains and their story; but, like Glendalough, the charm of the place does not depend wholly upon these. The lover of the beautiful can indulge his passion here, and find ample satisfaction. Standing on the ruined cathedral tower, or strolling along the edge of the rock which slopes abruptly away from the observer's feet, a magnificent expanse of country stretches out before him. His eye ranges over one of the most fertile tracts of Ireland, the Golden Vale of Tipperary. Away to the north is the beautiful river scene where stands Holy Cross Abbey, on the banks of the Suir; and further beyond, the town of Thurles, and the Devil's Bit Mountain, the spot whence the Prince of Darkness, according to popular tradition, snapped the Rock of Cashel in a fit of hunger and weariness, but soon dropped it in disgust. To the south are the rich lands of Tipperary, lying warm and luxuriant in the sunshine, having a superb background in the distant Galty Mountains; while in the western distance are the summits of the Slieve Phelim hills, beyond which is the busy town of Limerick. It is a scene upon which the delighted eye loves to linger, and which, when once enjoyed under favourable conditions, lives long in the memory. And if, under

THE CROSS OF CASHEL.

the influence of so much and such rich natural beauty, one tends to forget
the past, and to rejoice only in the happy present, the past which is so
powerfully represented on the Rock asserts itself even in the landscape, for
as the eye returns from the peaks of the Galty Mountains, or from the rich
colouring of the distant plain, it falls upon the ruined towers and arches of
Hore Abbey, which rise in the immediate foreground, and carry the thoughts
back once again to the men and the life of five centuries ago.

After leaving Cashel there is not much of very special interest until
Cork is reached. From the train fine views of the Galty Mountains are
obtained, especially in the early part of the year, when the snow is lying in

GENERAL VIEW OF CORK.
(From a photograph by Lawrence, of Dublin.)

the gullies, and crowning the summits. But for the most part the gently
undulating country is devoid of attractiveness. Queenstown, Youghal, and
Kilcolman are places that make demands upon the attention, and as they
are all easily reached from Cork, we may best visit them after we have
seen that city.

The metropolis of Southern Ireland is a city of 80,000 inhabitants, well
situated on the banks and in the valley of the Lee. It is a great port, and
also the centre of the butter trade for South-western Ireland. Provisions
and grain are also exported in considerable quantities. There are many
evidences of trade and busy life in the city; but there are also those signs

of depression so common in Irish towns. Empty and ruined houses may be seen in or near the main thoroughfares; and, busy as the streets and wharves undoubtedly are, they yet do not convey the impression of being utilized up to the full measure of possibility.

Cork produces strangely mixed impressions upon the stranger. Looked at as a whole from one of the heights commanding the city, the impression is pleasing. Some of the streets, as for example, the Grand Parade, George's Street, the South Mall, and Patrick Street are fine wide thoroughfares, filled with well-stocked shops, handsome buildings, and well-dressed people intent upon business. The quays and the bridges, six in number, are also fine and commodious, the most noteworthy being St. Patrick's and Parnell's, the latter a fine swivel bridge, opened in 1882. But many of the other streets are narrow, irregularly built, and not at all inviting to the passer-by. Still Cork ought to be estimated as a great sea-port, and judged on these lines it is perhaps ungracious to find much fault.

The city possesses some very handsome buildings, notably the Cathedral of St. Fin Barre, which stands on the site of an ancient monastery, and was consecrated in 1870. This magnificent building is an example of what can be done by the energy of one man. The late bishop, John Gregg, obtained the money, laid the foundation stone, consecrated the building, and arose from his bed, only a few weeks before his death, to place the top stones upon the towers and the spire. The Roman Catholic Cathedral is a handsome structure, and Trinity Presbyterian Church is one of the architectural ornaments of the town.

One of the Queen's Colleges is situated in Cork. In the churchyard of St. Anne's at Shandon, lie the remains of Father Prout, near the spot he loved, and within sound of those bells of which he wrote :—

With deep affection
And recollection
I often think of
      These Shandon bells,
Whose sound so wild would,
In the days of childhood,
Fling round my cradle
      Their magic spells.
On this I ponder
Where'er I wander,
And thus grow fonder,
      Sweet Cork, of thee ;
With thy bells of Shandon
That sound so grand on
The pleasant waters
      Of the River Lee.

I've heard bells chiming
Full many a clime in,
Tolling sublime in
      Cathedral shrine,
While at a glib rate
Brass tongues would vibrate –
But all their music
      Spoke naught like thine ;
For memory dwelling
On each proud swelling
Of thy belfry knelling
      Its bold notes free,
Made the bells of Shandon
Sound far more grand on
The pleasant waters
      Of the River Lee.

The easiest, and in some respects the pleasantest, excursion from Cork is a visit to Queenstown, or, as it used to be called, the Cove of Cork. The most enjoyable way is to go by steamer, but the trip by rail affords good views of the finest scenery. For some miles the route lies along the river, which soon begins to widen out into a very fine stream. On the north bank the land rises rapidly to a considerable elevation, and is very well wooded. The citizens of Cork have not been slow to avail themselves of the fine sites thus afforded for comfortable residences, and many fine houses adorn both the north and south shores. A conspicuous landmark upon the southern bank is Blackrock Castle, a modern building, situated upon a promontory at a bend in the river, which here turns sharply to the south, and broadens into a fine estuary. The railroad to Queenstown runs along the north shore, while the Cork and Passage railway occupies the southern.

Passing Carrigaloe and Monkstown, the steamer rounds a point and then enters one of the most commodious and also one of the loveliest harbours in the world. It is three miles long and two miles wide, and is completely landlocked, being entered by a channel two miles long and one wide. The expanse of water is broken by two islands, Haulbowline and Spike Island. The harbour runs east and west, and along its northern shore the town is built. The land rises abruptly to a height of several hundred feet, and a very easy climb will bring the visitor to one or other of many points of vantage. The enormous steamers of several of the Transatlantic lines call here, the harbour is generally busy with shipping, and seen under a sunny sky, few landscapes are so fair.

Six miles distant to the east is Cloyne, formerly the seat of an independent bishopric, but now associated with Cork. The famous philosopher Berkeley was Bishop of Cloyne from 1734 to 1753, and resided there for seventeen years. The glory of the town has departed; the old cathedral is used as a parish church, and there still stands a fine Round Tower, over 100 feet in height. Further still to the east, about twenty-six miles from Cork, is the town of Youghal, well situated on the hill overlooking the mouth of the Blackwater, the river whose valley forms one of the prettiest parts of Ireland. The town contains about 6,000 inhabitants, and is proud of its buildings and of its historical associations. The great church of St. Mary was for many years, like the Dublin cathedrals, in a ruinous state, and has, like them, been restored in recent years. A collegiate establishment was founded here by the Earl of Desmond in 1464, but the church dates back to the thirteenth century. The establishment consisted of a warden, eight fellows, and eight singing men, and the endowment was £600 a year. The house or college in which they resided is still in existence; but it is memorable from the fact that there once lived in it for several years a famous Englishman, Sir Walter Raleigh, and that he there entertained the great and gentle poet Edmund Spenser. The house retains few traces of its ancient appearance; it is rather an Elizabethan manor. It was repaired

H

in 1602 by Sir George Carew, and a few years later by Sir Richard Boyle, afterwards Earl of Cork, since it had been greatly injured in Desmond's rebellion. The interior is wainscoted with finely carved Irish oak. Tradition states that in the garden of this house Raleigh planted the first potato that grew in Ireland, and that under its yew-tree Spenser smoked the new and strange tobacco, and pondered *The Faerie Queene.* But it seems to have been too peaceful a home for the brilliant soldier and statesman, and although prominent for a time in the conduct of Irish affairs, his stay here was brief. Raleigh was present at the capture of Smerwick Fort in November, 1579; in 1584 he obtained the grant of a large tract of land in Munster; in 1589 he was again in Ireland, and on his return to England

SIR WALTER RALEIGH'S HOUSE, YOUGHAL (WITH BAY WINDOW OF HIS STUDY).

took Spenser with him, and introduced him to Queen Elizabeth. The same year saw the publication of the first three books of Spenser's masterpiece.

The Blackwater, like its Meath namesake, has a great reputation among the lovers of natural beauty. Following the river up some twenty or thirty miles, the Awbeg, one of the main tributaries, is reached. This stream is well known to anglers, and is noted for the fine trout it contains; it is also known to the readers of Elizabethan poetry as one of the streams described by Spenser in his *Colin Clout's Come Home Again,* which was penned in 1591, during his years of—to him—dreary banishment. The Mulla of this poem is the Awbeg of to-day:

Mulla, the daughter of Old Mole, so bright,
The nymph which of that watercourse has charge,
That, springing out of Mole, doth run downright
To Buttevant, where spreading forth at large
It giveth name unto that ancient city
Which Kil-ne-mullah cleped is of old,
Whose ragged ruins breed great ruth and pity
To travellers, which it from far behold.

About two miles to the north-west of Doneraile, a small town on the Awbeg, are the ruins of Kilcolman Castle, for ten years the home of Spenser. Judging from present appearance, it can never have been a

KILCOLMAN CASTLE. (*From a Photograph by Lawrence, of Dublin.*)

cheerful abode. It was a fairly strong keep, as every gentleman's house had to be in those stormy, troublous times; the rooms are small, and the arrangements for the comfort of the occupant seem to have been so necessarily imperfect that the visitor does not feel much desire for a return of those 'good old times,' at any rate if this should involve a return to such residences as the poet's home. This applies only to the castle itself, for the surroundings were very lovely. 'The castle,' writes Charles Smith, in his *Natural and Civil History of the County and City of Cork*, 'is now almost level with the ground, and was situated on the north side of a fine lake, in the midst of a vast plain, terminated to the east by the

H 2

county of Waterford mountains; Ballyhowra Hills to the north, or, as Spenser terms them, the Mountains of Mole, Nagle Mountains to the south, and the Mountains of Kerry to the west. It commanded a view of above half the breadth of Ireland; and must have been, when the adjacent uplands were wooded, a most pleasant and romantic situation.'

It was here that Spenser learned some of the deepest lessons of life. Driven into himself by the uncongenial nature of his surroundings, compelled to practise self-denial, he entered into fuller communion with the natural beauties around him. Here he passed through some of the uncertainties of a long but at the last successful wooing; and here he enjoyed the happiness of a married life based upon deep and ardent affection. Thus taught and thus disciplined, he learned those truths which he afterwards so beautifully expressed in his *Hymne of Heavenly Love*, in which the poet shows that he had learned the true secret of the Gospel. After describing how :

> Man, forgetful of his Master's grace,
> No less than angels, whom he did ensue,
> Fell from the hope of promised heavenly place
> Into the mouth of death, to sinners due,
> And all his offspring into thraldom threw,

and how the Lord Jesus Christ

> Out of the bosom of eternal blisse
> In which He reigned with His glorious Sire,
> He down descended, like a most demisse
> And abject thrall in flesh's frail attire,
> That He for him might pay Sin's deadly hire,
> And him restore unto that happy state
> In which he stood before his hapless fate.

the poet goes on to ask—

> How can we Thee requite for all this good?
> Or what can prize that Thy most precious blood?
>
> Yet nought Thou ask'st in lieu of all this love
> But love of us, for guerdon of Thy pain :
> Ay me! what can us lesse than that behove?
> Had He required life for us again,
> Had it been wrong to ask His owne with gain?
> He gave us life, He it restored lost;
> Then life were least, that us so little cost.
>
> But He our life hath left unto us free;
> Free that was thrall, and blessed that was banned :
> He aught demands but that we loving be,
> As He Himself hath loved us afore-hand,
> And bound thereto with an eternal band,
> Him first to love that was so dearly bought,
> And next our brethren, to His image wrought.

The years which Spenser passed at Kilcolman were among the most eventful in the whole course of English history. He came to Ireland in 1580 with the Deputy, Lord Grey de Wilton, and for about eight years he seems to have resided in or near Dublin. In all probability 1588 was the year in which he began his residence at Kilcolman. While he dreamed and chafed during these years of unwelcome banishment from England, Sidney died in Holland, the beautiful but wicked Mary Queen of Scots perished on the scaffold, the Armada came and was destroyed, and England emerged from her life and death conflict with Spain and the Papacy,

BLARNEY CASTLE. (*From a Photograph by Lawrence, of Dublin.*)

victorious and with such triumphant energy that she left mediævalism behind for ever, and took her place in the van of modern life and progress. Spenser felt most keenly the loss of his friend and typical hero, Sir Philip Sidney, and has enshrined his grief in noble verse. In the struggle known as Tyrone's Insurrection, Kilcolman Castle was attacked and burned, Spenser and his family escaping only with very great difficulty, and according to some accounts with the loss of an infant child, who was burned with the castle.

The easiest and the favourite excursion from Cork is to Blarney Castle, a spot which amply deserves the reputation it has acquired, although that reputation rests mainly upon the features of the place least worthy to sustain it. Multitudes know of or wish to touch the Blarney Stone, who are not so deeply impressed either by the picturesque splendour of the old ruin, or the exceeding beauty of its situation and surroundings. The castle stands upon a hillside which slopes steeply down to the River Blarney, a stream which winds through a lovely and well-wooded valley. Hard by is the neat little town, in which are several mills engaged in the manufacture of tweed.

The castle dates from the fifteenth century, and was founded by Cormac MacCarthy, who also founded the abbey and castle of Kilcrea, in the former of which he was buried. The castle and estates were forfeited in 1689, the last of the original owners being allowed a pension of £300.

Seen across the river by the approach from the town, the lofty grey mass of the huge quadrangular keep towering above the foliage of the trees, the castle presents a very imposing appearance.

The real Blarney Stone was one containing the inscription *Cormac Mac Carthy fortis me fieri fecit A.D.* The situation of the stone has shown a tendency to vary according to the predilections of the guides. But that now exhibited is the lowermost of those clasped between the iron bars, as shown in the engraving. Whatever the origin of the tradition, and of the custom of kissing the Blarney Stone, the reputation it has acquired of recent years has been due largely to Father Prout's verses.

There is a stone there,
That whoever kisses,
Oh ! he never misses
To grow eloquent.
'Tis he may clamber
To a lady's chamber,
Or become member
Of Parliament.
A clever spouter
He'll sure turn out, or
An out and outer
" To be let alone " !
Don't hope to hinder him
Or to bewilder him,
Sure he's a pilgrim
From the Blarney Stone.

The groves of Blarney,
They look so charming,
Down by the purlings
Of sweet silent brooks,
All decked by posies
That spontaneous grow there
Planted in order
In the rocky nooks.
'Tis there the daisy,
And the sweet carnation,
The blooming pink,
And the rose so fair ;
Likewise the lily
And the daffadowndilly—
All flowers that scent
The sweet open air.

But rich as this whole district is in pretty scenery and interesting sites, we cannot extend our consideration of them. Only a passing mention can be made of the western part of County Cork. Those who can make time and opportunity should certainly visit Kinsale, Bandon, Clonakilty, Dunmanway and Skibbereen.

THE UPPER LAKE OF KILLARNEY.

GLENGARIFF.

CHAPTER V.

GLENGARIFF, KILLARNEY, AND VALENTIA.

THERE are three main routes from Cork to Killarney. The tamest is by rail viâ Mallow ; the most adventurous is by rail to Macroom, and thence to Killarney by the north road, as it is called, one of the finest drives in South-western Ireland, running through the country of the MacCarthys, with their ruined castles, and enabling the traveller to see Gougane Barra and the Pass of the Deer. The former is a lonely lake, lying embosomed in a great hollow formed by the mountains, which tower in parts almost perpendicularly above it. In the centre of the lake is an islet sacred to St. Finn Bar, which was for ages the object of special pilgrimages. The scenery here, for wild magnificence and power to touch the imagination, can hold its own with any in this region—so full of grand mountain and lake solitudes. The Pass of the Deer is a deep mountain cleft about two miles in length, 'the most sternly grand defile in Ireland, a scene of utter loneliness, where no song of bird or hum of bee breaks the monotonous stillness, save where the ripple of numerous sparkling rills course down the side of the acclivities. There are immense masses of rock seemingly poised in the air, almost perpendicularly on either side, clothed with stunted arbutus, rowan-tree, yew and holly, while huge projecting cliffs ever and anon seem threatening to bar the visitor's progress.' Here the outlawed O'Sullivans and O'Learys long defied the Government, and in 1822 the adherents of Captain Rock for a long time held possession of the pass, until dislodged by Lord Bantry and the military. It is a district well adapted for lawlessness of this kind.

But the popular route is by way of Bantry and Glengariff. This takes the traveller along one of the roads in Ireland most frequented, at least in the tourist season ; but it also has compensations, inasmuch as it offers some most magnificent drives, and at the chief stopping points some of the very best hotels in Ireland are to be found. A short but pleasant railway journey from Cork enables the visitor to see the pretty country on the road to Bandon, to catch a good passing glimpse of that well-situated town, to see something of the wildest parts of County Cork, and finally brings him to Bantry, at the head of the famous bay of the same name. Here, if disposed to stop, he will find very comfortable accommodation, and although the little town presents an ancient appearance, and has a fish-like odour, there is nothing in it that need detain him long. But with the drive to Glengariff the beauties of this region begin to reveal themselves. The road winds along the north-eastern · shores of Bantry Bay, which are somewhat hilly, affording consequently beautiful and ever-varying views. Whether the drive be taken in the full light of the midday sun, or when the softer lights and the shadows of evening are over the landscape, it will linger long in the memory. The noble expanse of the bay, the lofty peaks of the Sugar Loaf and other distant mountains, the fine bold rock contours, the little streams that ripple down from the surrounding mountains, the splendid colourings of sea and sky and rock and heath, all combine to heighten the enjoyment of the traveller. Especially fine are the views when the approach of evening tends to deepen the shadows and to robe the more distant prospects in a lovely purple haze.

Eloquent descriptions of Glengariff abound, sometimes accurate and adequate, sometimes charged with a pardonable exaggeration. But the perusal of these tends to form either untrue or disproportionate ideas of this celebrated glen. Perhaps the ideal course would be to go and see the spot, and then read the descriptions. Glengariff is emphatically a place where the eye sees what it is capable of seeing, and the impression received will vary here, more than in most places, according to the brain to which the eye transmits its sensations. Those who love the combination of bold rocks with lovely dells whose sides are fringed with beautiful trees, and through which musically murmuring streams run down to the sea ; those who rejoice in the fresh, blue, health-giving ocean, and who yet love to look upon it in its gentler and softer moods; those who like when taking a holiday to exchange the rush and struggle and selfishness of modern metropolitan life for the peaceful country, far removed from the roar of business and the fierceness of modern competition, and yet sufficiently in touch with the outer world to avoid all traces of stagnation—such as these can hardly do better than select Glengariff as a place of resort. The modern tourist loves his comforts, and these he can have in the hotels. Be he pedestrian, or cyclist, or fisherman, or sketcher, or lover of boating and driving, here can he indulge to the full his favourite recreation. And he can at the same time breathe some of the purest air and rejoice in the marvellous wealth of rich and lovely scenery with which the beneficent Creator has gladdened this part of the land.

The name Glengariff means 'the rugged glen.' It includes the harbour formed by the innermost recess of Bantry Bay, and the valley through which flows the Glengariff River, in its descent from Eagle's Nest Mountain, to the sea. The bay is dotted with a large number of tiny islets; the river rushes headlong down from its source, reaching its highest point of beauty, perhaps, at the old ruined arches of what is known as Cromwell's Bridge. The temperature in this favoured glen varies within narrow limits, the vegetation is rich, the arbutus, the rowan-tree, the holly, azaleas, rhododendrons, and hydrangeas, all flourish here, and its wonderful combination of beauties and advantages make it a notable place of rest for the overworked and weary, and a choice wintering place for the delicate.

But most who visit this earthly Paradise, like ourselves, however fain to linger, have to hasten on to other scenes. There is a road from Glengariff to Gougane Barra, and thence to Killarney; but the vast majority go by the main road to Kenmare. This is as fine a drive as any tourist need wish to enjoy. The road runs through the village, and then for a short distance along the left bank of the Glengariff River, and finally begins to wind ever higher and higher up the valley of a small tributary of the Glengariff River, which it finally crosses, and winds around a bold, steep hill at a height of nearly 800 feet above the sea. From this point a comprehensive view of the greater part of Bantry Bay is obtained. It then turns sharply to the north, rising still higher and penetrating into ever wilder mountain scenery, until a peak known as Turner's Rock, over 1,300 feet above the sea, is reached. This is pierced by a fine tunnel, and as the car passes out of the long and somewhat gloomy passage a superb view greets him. Stretched out before him, but mainly to his left hand, are the fine multitudinous peaks of Ireland's greatest mountain chain, the McGillicuddy Reeks. Seen early in the year, say in April, they are often covered with snow, and present a most beautiful appearance. Seen under any circumstances with the essential element of a tolerably clear

McGILLICUDDY REEKS.

atmosphere, their wild forms, their great extent, their fine configurations rejoice the heart within the lover of natural beauty. The road climbs for a time along the steep side of one of these huge mountain masses, and gradually descends, crosses the river, and finally runs for miles along the left bank of the Sheen. The scenery gets softer as one approaches Kenmare. The Sheen finally empties into the Sound, the inner part of Kenmare Bay, and, about a mile below the mouth of the Sheen, a fine suspension bridge has been thrown across Kenmare Bay, over which passes the road.

Kenmare is quite a recent town compared with some of its neighbours, having been founded as a colony in 1670 by Sir William Petty, the ancestor of the present Lansdowne family. There is little in it to detain the visitor, unless he intends to explore the fine mountainous country round about, in which case it becomes a very convenient headquarters. For most the hour or two of waiting for the mail-cart, or securing a fresh horse and car, is sufficient; and after a brief stay the journey to Killarney is begun.

Kenmare is nearly on the sea level, and the road soon begins to ascend. It winds along the base of the mountains, rising higher and higher, until it crosses the top of Windy Pass, at an elevation of about 1,000 feet above the sea. It then skirts the slopes high above the Dwenregh River, runs by the northern margin of Looscaunagh Lough, skirts the base of a small mountain, and then affords the traveller what is considered to be, and justly so, the very finest view of the Killarney Lakes in all their variety and extent. From this point, until Killarney is reached, wherever the eye turns it meets fine peaks, waters gleaming in the sunshine, enticing glens that look as if specially created to afford picnic facilities, and the ever-changing expressions of natural beauty which, if not unrivalled, are worthy of the highest praise, and capable of affording very pure pleasure.

And here again it should be noted that Killarney suffers most from its friends. Some of these, not content to allow its claims to rest upon the evidence of a very high type of beauty, clearly manifest to any one capable of judging, make monstrous claims, and give expression to absurd and high-flown descriptions, which only tend to irritate and to provoke comparisons that are better not made at all. Killarney, in the writer's judgment, is quite capable of holding its rank among the districts of exceptional natural beauty; but for its admirers to expect those who visit it to admit that it stands without a rival, can only lead to vexation of spirit.

Arrived at Killarney, the first task is to see it. At present the arrangements for doing this are not so convenient as they might be. Those who come by the Kenmare Road get a succession of lovely distant views, and those whose purses admit of a sojourn at the Lake or the Royal Victoria Hotels have no reason to complain; but for all others, to get anything like a view of the lakes is a task involving the expenditure of time, exertion, and money. The domain of the Earl of Kenmare lies between Lough Leane and the town, and around this a lofty wall has been constructed, with the result that it prevents any view whatsoever, unless the visitor proceeds to some such recognised point of vantage as Ross Castle. It is the same on the road to Muckross Abbey. In fact, it is possible, or rather, as there is no choice in the matter, it is compulsory, on all who wish to travel the six miles of road between Muckross Abbey and Lake View House, to journey by a road which on one side of the way presents the unvarying monotony of a blank stone wall. The patient endurance of those who thus journey is not strengthened by the recollection that on the other side of the wall are some of the best views in what is considered to be the loveliest region in Ireland. Whether, if these walls were lowered, matters would be better, the experts must decide. It is quite certain, even if the trees on the various estates and the distance from the water prevents any view of the lake or the surrounding mountains, that the mental irritation produced upon all who have to pass along the five or six miles of dead wall would be avoided, without in any way interfering with the rights or security of the fortunate possessors of the northern and eastern shores of Lough Leane, if this could be done.

Killarney is a district rather than a town. There is indeed a cluster of streets, lined for the most part by very unattractive houses and shops, and not at all remarkable for neatness. These constitute the town, but no visitor

Ross Castle, Killarney.

is likely to wish to linger here. But the country about, for fifteen miles or so, especially to the south and west, abounds in peaks that may be ascended, mountain loughs, about which linger grim legends, waterfalls and cascades, passes and glens, trips by car or by boat—in fact, scenery, the chief beauties of which can be exhausted in two days, or which can afford the careful explorer pleasant tasks for weeks.

The most comprehensive excursion is to the Gap of Dunloe and back by way of the lakes. For this a whole day is needed, and the earlier the start the better. A good pedestrian can walk it, but the pleasantest way is to take a car to the foot of the Gap; by this means the five miles of wall are passed quickly, and the wayfarer is fresh for the walk through the Gap, and any excursion that may seem desirable, say the ascent of Purple Mountain, or a stroll up the Black Valley. By this route the Killorglin road is taken, and on the right hand, two or three miles out of the town, the ruins of Aghadoe Church and Round Tower are passed. About two miles or so away from the mouth of the Gap, the first experience of the great Killarney nuisance is encountered. Not far from Aghadoe the road forks, and here, on the alert to catch their victims early, are stationed a collection of the Killarney beggars, misnamed guides. They are mounted on ponies, and their object is to succeed in getting these taken for the ride up the pass. There is no escape from them, and even the plan of engaging one for the purpose of stalling off the others is defeated by the additional swarms that are encountered in the pass. The best plan is to say little or nothing, to buy nothing, and, above all, to drink none of the various mixtures that are offered every few hundred yards along the route. It is really intolerable that these hordes of beggars should be allowed thus to detract from the enjoyment of a very lovely district. But as things are, there seems to be no remedy. One is inclined to hold that if the advocates of Home Rule could make it evident that their panacea would banish the beggars, not only from the Gap, but from all the other lovely parts of the kingdom, they would at once secure the sympathy of all travellers. These would consent to a good deal in order to secure the disappearance of the men and boys who offer ponies for hire, who bring cornets to wake the echoes, and who wish to fire off cannons that look admirably adapted to destroy the individual bold enough to fire them ; together with the girls who offer for sale woollen socks and potheen and milk, the whole tribe of Kate Kearney's descendants who sell deplorable photographs of themselves and the huts in which they live, and the miscellaneous crew who look upon every visitor as the possibility of a copper or a sixpence.

The Gap of Dunloe is a pass between the Toomies and the McGilli-cuddy Reeks, up which any but the feeblest walkers can go with the utmost ease, from the point where the cars always stop. The River Loe traverses the Gap, expanding at intervals into five lakes. A good road winds up the valley, crossing the stream by bridges in two places. The mountains rise very steeply to a height of over 2,000 feet, and the scenery is very wild. The narrowness of the defile combined with the height of the mountains gives it a sombre and awe-inspiring influence. At one point the ravine narrows, and a huge mass of rock has fallen and split into two irregular portions. The road runs between these enormous stones, which have the semblance of a rude gateway. The spot is known as The Pike. The

THE PIKE.

impression of wildness and desolation is considerably weakened, not
only by the troops of beggars, but more
legitimately by the number of little farms
in the valley, and by the numerous traces
of fairly prosperous agriculture. As the
ascent is made, very good views to the
north are obtained, but by far the finest is enjoyed when the summit of the
pass is reached, and the traveller stands with the beautiful Owenreach Valley
at his feet, the many-islanded Upper Lake to his left, the Kenmare Road
and the Police Barracks directly opposite, and the Black Valley to the right

over which tower the rugged pinnacles of the Reeks. Occasionally one meets with absurdly over-drawn descriptions of this Black Valley. When the writer saw it, under a bright April sun, it failed signally to harmonize with its name, since it lay smilingly at his feet, looking most attractive in its beauty.

By an easy road the descent into the valley is made, Lord Brandon's cottage is passed—a toll of one shilling being levied on every visitor—and then the boat is taken for the row down to Ross Island. This is certainly

THE EAGLE's NEST, KILLARNEY.

not less enjoyable than the earlier half of the excursion. If any part of Killarney deserves the palm, it is this row along the placid waters of the Upper Lake, in and out among its many rocky islets, and down the Long Range which connects the Upper and Middle Lakes. To the south rise Cromaglan and Torc Mountains, to the north the spurs of Purple Mountain and the Eagle's Nest. The views are extremely beautiful, and there is a marvellous variety of colouring and of contour. The boatmen, in their well-meant efforts to amuse, talk a considerable amount of arrant nonsense about the uses to which the ever-present O'Donoghue puts the many

I

strangely-shaped rocks which abound on every hand. The most effective view of all is where the boat, following as it must the windings of the stream, passes immediately beneath the loftiest part of the Eagle's Nest. This mountain, like its neighbours, is clad for some hundreds of feet above

THE OLD WEIR BRIDGE, KILLARNEY.

the water level with arbutus, ash, oak, holly and other trees. Among other charms, this spot possesses a fine echo.

Soon after passing this point the great excitement of shooting the rapid at the Old Weir Bridge occurs. There is just sufficient fall to impart a somewhat lively motion to the boat, and the distance is so short that almost before you are aware the descent has begun it is over.

INNISFALLEN, KILLARNEY.

Under exceptional circumstances, with the water unusually high, it is conceivable that the passage would be attended with some risk. Of course

none but those well acquainted with the peculiarities of the place should
attempt to take a boat down ; the regular boatmen are all more than equal
to the not very anxious demands which the descent makes upon their nerve
and skill.

After shooting the bridge, the boat glides into a most lovely part, the
Meeting of the Waters, and the shore of Dinis Island, which divides the
stream, one portion of the waters flowing out into the Middle or Torc
Lake, the other passing on to Lough Leane.

Dinis Island is delightful, and any who have neither time nor inclination for the longer trips will find this part most accessible, and equal in
beauty to any in the whole range of the Killarney lakes.

Passing under Brickeen Bridge, having tarried for a moment to gather
a sprig or two of arbutus, the boat shoots out upon the wide waters of
the Lower Lake. This is 5,000 acres in extent, being, roughly speaking,
5½ miles long by 2½ wide. When it is breezy, as the writer tested by
experience, the waves can rise, and the rowers need to bend their backs to
the oars to urge their craft across to Innisfallen and then on to Ross Island.
The former, 21 acres in extent, is the gem of Lough Leane. It is lovely
as regards its scenery, and it is venerable by reason of past associations.
Here, in the seventh century, St. Finian founded a monastery, of which some
traces have come down to us ; and here one of the famous early records of
Irish history, the Annals of Innisfallen, were penned. At Ross Castle we
land ; the engraving on page 110 enables the reader to realize what manner
of ruin it is. On the mainland, opposite the Tomies' side of Innisfallen,
is O'Sullivan's Cascade, which consists of three distinct falls, one of the
favourite shorter excursions. At the south-eastern end of Lough Leane is
the ruined Muckross Abbey. It was founded, according to Ware, by Donald
MacCarthy about 1440 ; but the Annals of the Four Masters record that
it dates from 1340 ; there is some evidence that the building was begun by
Teige, and finished in 1440 by his son Donald. It was restored, as an
inscription on the north side of the choir states, in 1626. 'The church
consists of a nave and choir, separated by a belfry of small proportions,
and only calculated to hold a single bell. This belfry is pierced by a
narrow arch, which connects the nave and choir. On the south side of the
nave there is a small chapel or transept, with which it is connected by a
large archway ; and on the north side a small doorway leads into the
cloisters, which is the most perfect and interesting portion of the building.
It is a square of twelve yards, encompassed by an arcade lighting the
surrounding corridor, which is about five feet in length. The arcade consists
of ten semicircular arches in its north and east sides, and twelve pointed
ones on the south and west. The pillars and mouldings are of grey marble.
The effect of these cloisters is rendered singularly solemn and imposing by
a venerable and majestic yew-tree, which rises like a stately column from

the centre of the enclosure, and which, from the density of the dark green foliage of its spreading branches, permits but a "dim, religious light" to penetrate the area. The stem of this remarkable tree, which there is no reason to doubt is coeval with the abbey, is upwards of twelve feet in height, and about six feet six inches in circumference.

'The vault of the MacCarthy Mores is placed in the centre of the choir, and is marked by a flat stone level with the floor, on which the coronet and arms of the Earl of Glencare are rudely sculptured; a more stately monument, as represented in the illustration, marks the grave of O'Donoghue of the Glens, who died in 1808, and is buried in the same vault.' [1]

Hard by Muckross Abbey the road to Mangerton, the loftiest mountain near Killarney, 2,576 feet high, turns off from the Kenmare Road. It is a very easy ascent, and the view 'is superb, embracing in the east Crohane, the Paps, Cahirbarnagh, and all that extensive country lying between Millstreet, Mallow and Tipperary, with the blue range of the Galtys in the far distance. Northward and to the west is Tralee, with the Slievemish Mountains in the neighbourhood of Dingle and Ventry, while a faint white line in the horizon marks the north estuary of the Shannon as it flows past Tarbert and Kilrush. Due west are the Torc, the Purple Mountain, and the

THE CHOIR OF MUCKROSS ABBEY.

Reeks, with Castlemaine Haven and the Laune running at their feet; to the south is an immense sea of hills occupying the district towards Kenmare. The Bays of Kenmare and Bantry are prominent objects in this view—a view which can never be blotted out from memory. At the foot lie the Lakes of Killarney in all their beauty, with the thick wood and groves encircling their shores.' [2]

[1] *Dublin Penny Journal*, vol. i., p. 410.   [2] *Murray's Handbook for Ireland*, p. 317.

At a steep part of the ascent, about three-quarters of the way up, is a depression in the mountain, from which the cliffs rise up steeply, and occupied by a tarn. This depression is known as the Devil's Punch Bowl, and from it descends one of the streams which form the Torc Waterfall. This is a fine fall, some sixty feet in height, situated in a ravine called Owengariff. It is most easily reached from Killarney by the Kenmare Road.

Having enjoyed the lovely scenery of Killarney, no traveller who can spare the time should fail to visit Valentia. By this trip some of the most interesting and characteristic portions of Kerry are to be seen, notably what is known as the Mountain Drive, along the southern shores of Dingle Bay, Glenbeagh, late of eviction notoriety, Valentia Island, and, above all, the coast with its islands, pre-eminent among these being the Skelligs. It is possible to go from Killarney to Killorglin by train, and thence by omnibus or car to Cahirsiveen. But the best way for any one who wishes to see typical men and things is to go by mail-car. In many parts of Ireland these most con-

A KERRY CABIN AND ITS INHABITANTS.

venient conveyances run. They are not luxurious, their cushions are often hard and well-worn, they are not unfrequently heavily laden with parcel-post impedimenta and other mail baggage; and he who travels by them must be prepared to rough it a little, and to be considered possibly a trifle plebeian in his tastes. But for all these things there are ample compensations. They are fast; they are cheap; each car has a driver thoroughly familiar with the country he traverses, and almost invariably civil, obliging, and communicative; the passengers are generally typical peasants, and all along the route little incidents happen, slight in themselves, but of peculiar interest oftentimes to the observant traveller, because

TORC WATERFALL, KILLARNEY.

they enable him to see the people as they are in themselves, and while engaged in their daily avocations. Just as the ordinary Norwegian steamer is a better conveyance for those who wish to study that interesting people, than the special tourist vessels that run to the North Cape, so the mail-car gives many a trait, life-study, amusing incident, or friendly chat, utterly unknown to those who journey in Ireland only by special car or by tourist-crowded coach or omnibus.

But he who goes from Killarney to Valentia by mail-car has to get up early. It is timed to leave the post-office at 5.30 A.M., and does so, unless detained by the mail-train being late, a state of affairs which the writer knows by experience occasionally happens. This particular route is traversed daily by a 'long car,' that is, one that needs two horses, can carry about a dozen passengers and a heavy load of mail. The first stage is to Killorglin, about thirteen miles, and after the northern end of Lough Leane has been passed, on the left hand the Reeks present a series of exceedingly fine mountain views. From a broad expanse of morass and bog they rise rapidly and boldly, the lower slopes being rounded and massive, but the upper peaks exhibiting a series of wild and craggy pinnacles. Killorglin has nothing attractive about it, except its fine situation above the Launc, which is here crossed by a bridge leading to Milltown and Castlemaine. Beyond Killorglin the road rises by a long ascent, which gradually brings into view Dingle Bay and the range of hills along its northern shore. Six miles on a steep descent, along the valley of the Caragh, leads to Caragh Bridge, which crosses a wild mountain stream rushing down from Lough Caragh. The district does not belie its appearance; it is a noted spot for salmon and trout fishing. Passing through Glenbeagh, the road gradually ascends, and, on turning the shoulder of a hill, a splendid view of Dingle Bay is obtained, and for miles the car runs along the face of the slope high above the sea level. The mountains of Clare on the further shore of the bay are all in full view. Perhaps the chief draw-back is the singular absence of shipping, hardly a fishing-boat even being in sight. Leaving the sea, a broad valley is traversed, with mountains on either side, and, crossing Carhan Bridge, Cahirsiveen comes into view. Close to the bridge is a ruined house, of which part of the walls, overgrown with ivy, remain. Here the renowned Daniel O'Connell was born. Cahirsiveen is a poor but apparently thriving little town. It lies embosomed in a bold mountainous country. It is 38 miles from Killarney, and few mail-car rides in Ireland so well repay the fatigue involved in their accomplishment.

Valentia Island, or rather the ferry, is three miles beyond Cahirsiveen The island is separated from the mainland by a strait half a mile broad. The engraving gives two views. In the circle is depicted the view from Valentia pier; it is identical with that obtained from the windows of the hotel, which is so placed as to face the pier. In the extreme right is seen the house on

VALENTIA.

(From photographs by Lawrence, of Dublin.)

the mainland from which
the ferryboat starts. The
other picture represents
Knights Town as seen
by the wayfarer about to
make the passage. The broad
strait forming Valentia Harbour, the mountain, the many tones
of brown on the hills, the clear
sky, the fine colours of the water, combine to make this a scene upon
which the eye lingers with delight. In the extreme left of the larger
engraving a little cluster of houses is shown. This is the headquarters
of the celebrated Atlantic Telegraph Company. The second building
from the left is the house in which the instruments are kept busy
day and night constantly receiving and transmitting messages across the
Atlantic. The company now possesses three cables, one of which is in
direct communication with Embden, in North Germany, by which continental messages are sent direct viâ Newfoundland and Cape Breton to
New York. The public are admitted at stated hours, but the writer, by
courtesy of the secretary of the London office, was allowed to inspect the
premises during the busiest part of the day. The instruments occupy two
rooms. In one the operators are engaged with the Embden cable, some
transmitting messages to America; others to various parts of the Continent
viâ Embden. The messages are expressed in all languages, and in various

ciphers. As the operator reads the message which is being spelled out by the instrument he transmits it to Newfoundland, and this is so promptly done that the first half of a message is across the ocean before the other has entirely left Germany. In the second room Stock Exchange work, press messages and private telegrams are coming and going. When the writer saw this room four operators were hard at work on the Stock Exchange messages, all in cipher. The superintendent stated that a New York broker is apt to grow impatient if he cannot get a message through to London and a reply in the course of a few minutes! Competition has so increased the companies that the rates are very low; but the low rates have not correspondingly increased the traffic. Although 3,000 messages pass through in twenty-four hours, on the average, this is by no means the maximum that could be dealt with, and meanwhile the shareholders of this company, the pioneers in ocean telegraph work, have to be content with one per cent. dividend. The officials and clerks form a little colony in this extreme south-western nook of Ireland.

The hotel at Knights Town is very comfortable and reasonable, and any visitor tired of such tourist-frequented regions as Killarney or the Causeway, wishing to spend a few days in some breezy, health-giving resort 'far from the madding crowd,' might do very much worse than visit Valentia Island. Bathing, boating, and fishing are all to be had; there are plenty of short excursions; and when the wish to go further afield comes, it is not difficult to sail across to Dingle, and although it is a somewhat formidable trip, it is by no means impossible, as we shall proceed to show, to get out to the Great Skellig, which is by far the most interesting island off the Irish coast.

The Skelligs are three rocky islets forming the most south-westerly extensions of the kingdom of Ireland. The strong light perched on a ledge of the Great Skellig, shining out clear and powerful over sixteen or twenty miles of the heaving Atlantic, is the first sign of land that the traveller from the west sees. Though inhabited now only by the light-keepers and their families, centuries ago a monastery flourished there, and no extant remains in Ireland enable us to picture the old monastic life of the early Irish Church better than those which still crown the lofty top of the Great Skellig.

It was long the writer's desire to visit this famous spot, and this desire was not lessened by the discovery that the trip was not easy to accomplish, and that the intending visitor was here, more than in most spots along this coast, at the mercy of wind and weather. Unless these were very propitious, the attempt to land was certain to result in failure. But wind and weather were in a kindly mood towards him on the one occasion when he found himself at Valentia with a day to spare; and no single day's excursion has ever afforded him fuller gratification.

The nearest village to the Skelligs on the mainland is Port Magee, a little fishing station on the strait separating the southern coast of Valentia Island from the mainland.   It is from this place that, at the time of writing (1888), the boat carrying supplies and letters to the lighthouse on the rock sails at irregular intervals.   It is possible to arrange for a visit in this boat, but it is more satisfactory in most cases to hire one specially for the excursion.   The Great Skellig is a sharp-pointed mass of rock, rising straight up from the bosom of the Atlantic, and situated about 9 miles to the

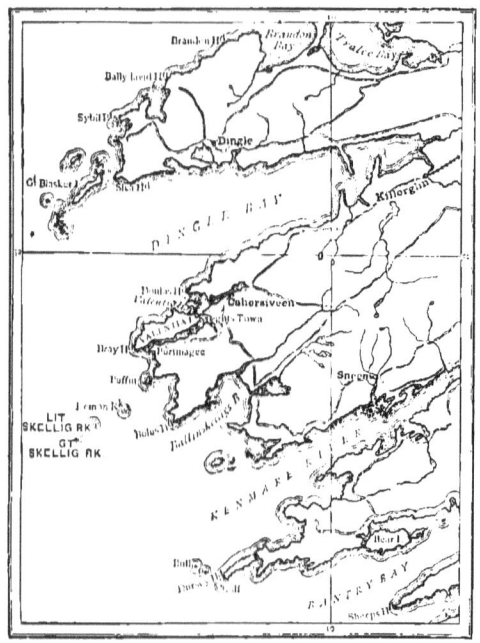

south-west of Port Magee. It is a most enjoyable expedition for those who are not afflicted with nervousness, and who can sit for hours in a small boat as she rides upon the mighty Atlantic swell, and receive therefrom nothing but benefit and enjoyment.   It is emphatically a trip to be avoided by the timid, by those subject to sea-sickness, and, unless under very exceptional circumstances, by ladies.

Perhaps some adequate impression of the interest of such a trip, and of the Skelligs themselves, can best be conveyed to the reader by describing the author's excursion thither.   It fell upon an April day, the only one that could be spared for the adventure.   On awaking at 6.30 A.M.—and he who would see the Skelligs should be early on the road—the eye was gladdened by the sight of brilliant sunshine.   A jaunting car soon traversed the seven miles that intervene between Knights Town and the ferry over against Port Magee.   A very ancient mariner conveys passengers across, and then a certain amount of bargaining secured a boat and a crew of four fine muscular young fishermen for the trip out and back to the Skelligs. The scale of payment was determined to some extent by their assurance that it would be necessary in the state of the wind and weather on that particular day to row probably the whole way there, and certainly the whole way back. And their forecast proved true.

And here it may be remarked that no one, from economical or other reasons, should attempt this trip without *at least* four men. Even in the best weather the landing upon the rock is a somewhat delicate operation, and no boat should ever start which is not in itself capable of standing very rough weather, and so manned that if caught in a breeze there should be ample strength to do all that is needful. Whether I paid more or less than usual I am unable to say. I hired the boat and the four men for the day at a charge of twenty-five shillings, and when they landed me safe and sound in the evening, I felt they had well earned their money.

We rowed away from the tiny pier at Port Magee about 10 A.M., and were soon at the mouth of the inlet upon which Port Magee is situated. There was a slight breeze from the north-east, the sun was shining, the sea had a steel-blue tint, the sky was clear, and as we drew near the mouth of the inlet the first taste of what was before us came. A broken ledge of rocks protects the mouth of the harbour. Within the sea was almost calm, but upon the ledge the Atlantic was breaking with a low, thunderous roar, which would not have been pleasing had not the wild foam looked so dazzlingly white in the sunshine, and so fascinated the eye with its ever-varying forms of beauty, that delight in the scene quite overpowered the nervous imagination of what might happen should one of those great rollers send our light boat against any of the thousand ugly pointed rocks so uncannily close to our side. A few minutes' hard rowing, and we were out upon the main. Turning a bold headland, we got our first view of the islets for which we were making. Away out on the ocean, sharply defined against the horizon, were two huge masses of rock, and most beautiful did they appear. Too far away to exhibit any of their inequalities of outline, they rose up from the sea like pyramids, and, enshrouded in an exquisite blue haze, they appeared like twin sapphires. Seen from the low elevation of the boat, lying peacefully on the far horizon, shining forth in their sapphire beauty, one could easily feel and appreciate how the Irish along this coast have acquired and cling to the belief that westwards are the Islands of the Blest, the land of plenty and of peace.

As the land receded we began to get a superb view of the coast, and a cruel coast it is. Successively Bray Head, Puffin Island, Bolus Head, the Great Blasquets, and many another headland and islet, came into view. The cliffs in many parts rise from three to six hundred feet, in some cases sheer from the water. But weird and fantastic in form as they often are, wherever the eye lights one impression is received, that of eternal strength. There is nothing of the curious frayed appearance presented by the horizontal strata of the cliffs further north. These rise up boldly, uncompromisingly, and you feel as you look upon them that here is a solidity and a strength

upon which even the Atlantic in its seasons of wildest fury can make no
impression.   It is in vain that his hugest billows dash against these
tremendous barriers.   In the conflict, ceaseless, yet fruitless, all softness
has disappeared.   They present a stern grey front, and in their quiet yet
awe-inspiring fixity they seem to say, 'Hitherto shalt thou come, but no
further, and here *shall* thy proud waves be stayed.'

We row on, and for two or three miles seem to be making little or no
headway.   But gradually the cliffs of the mainland recede, and we draw
near to the first of the group, that known as the Lemon Rock.   This is
a mass of rock rising only a few feet above high water mark.   It has been
worn into a ragged outline by the ceaseless action of the water, and as we
pass it so far away that the roar of the surge is softened by the distance,
we can see the spray shooting up
in columns of the purest white.

THE GANNET.

It seems to take a long while,
our crew rowing hard all the
time, to get beyond the Lemon
Rock.   But at last it is left
upon our port quarter, and
we have now done the larger
half of our outward journey.
We slowly cross the stretch
of two or three miles which
separate the Lemon Rock
from the Little Skellig.   One
feels afresh the insignificance
of man in the presence of
the great forces of nature.
The sun has now gone be-
hind the clouds, the sea has
changed to a cold grey, the
waves have risen a little, the boat seems small and frail, the ocean seems
wide and mighty.   There is no vessel within two or three miles of us, and
only five or six visible in the whole circuit of our horizon.   The strongest
swimmer, in case of need, could hardly hope to reach either the Skelligs or
the shore.   But a glance at the trim craft as she steadily surmounts wave
after wave, a look at the intelligent faces and sturdy arms of the rowers
as they cheerily urge on the boat, reassures us, and we banish all nervous
thoughts and give ourselves up to thorough enjoyment of an hour not likely
to recur in a lifetime.

We pass near the Little Skellig, and while doing so have ample time
to study the large numbers of gannets clustering upon the broken ledges of
its most southern haunt in Great Britain.   The sea is running strongly

THE GREAT SKELLIG.

through a large natural arch at one of the sharp angles of the rock, and though we cannot help wishing for the sunlight, we can see clearly the weird forms into which the storms of ages have beaten its many cliffs and pinnacles.

But now all our attention is concentrated upon the main object of our trip. We are within a mile of the Great Skellig, and already it seems to tower high above us in solitary and mysterious grandeur. On all sides the cliff rises so abruptly and so forbiddingly from the sea that access seems impossible, and one feels curious to discover how and where it is possible to get a footing. As we pass under a tremendous shoulder of rock which forms the base of the peak running up almost perpendicularly for about 700 feet above the sea, a little cove comes into view. Comparatively calm as the day is, and assured as we are by the boatmen that there could not be a finer day for landing, it is evident even to an inexperienced eye that the sea is running in the cove in a way that shows what careful handling the boat needs. By skilful management one of the crew is enabled to jump upon a ledge of rock made exceedingly slippery by sea-weed growing upon it. But it is not the first time he has set foot upon the Great Skellig. I follow, and am kept from any risk of a fall by his stalwart arm, and then, by an admirable arrangement of ropes, the boat, after the others have landed, is swung so that she rides up and down in the middle of the cove with no risk of coming against any one of the numerous rocks which would soon knock a hole in her.

And here we are, after our three hours' pull, safely landed upon the famous islet. A very fine road, which was made by government labour in the early part of this century, has been cut out of the perpendicular cliff, and winds slowly up to the lighthouse. It affords here and there splendid views of the cliffs in its gradual ascent, and at one point crosses over a chasm. Being on the lee side of the island, when we saw it, and the sea as quiet probably as it ever is there, the swell as it rolled in was pleasant to the ear and the eye; but in a westerly gale the scene here must be terrific. As one stands upon this road, clinging closely to the face of the rock, and looks westward; remembering that the nearest land in that direction is nearly 2,000 miles away, a sense of isolation comes over the mind.

Until recent years there were two lighthouses upon the island, but now only one is in use. This is the lower one, well and securely placed upon a platform levelled in the rock about 140 feet above the sea. But even at this altitude it is not altogether free from serious assault on the part of the ocean. A few years ago the roof was partly carried away by an enormous wave hurled against it by one of those severe gales that from time to time sweep across the Atlantic. The whole western side of the islet has been beaten by the waves into precipitous cliff.

The only human beings at present resident upon the island are the

K

lighthouse keeper with his wife and children, and his assistant. There is just enough space upon the upper part of the island for the children to run about and for a few sheep to graze. But the monotony of such a life must be very great, and it seems hard upon children that they should be compelled to spend two or three years of their young life on such a lonely, not to say dangerous rock. The lighthouse keeper here, in common with his brethren elsewhere, is courteous and willing to show all that there is to be seen. Perhaps his cordiality of greeting to the stranger is somewhat warmer than usual from the fact that a visit is indeed a rare event, and the sight of a strange face something to be remembered.

Lonely indeed is the Great Skellig, bracing the air, and picturesque the views afforded by its own rugged cliffs, and those of the Lesser Skellig, its only near neighbour; but these would hardly form sufficient attractions to draw the visitor, were it not for the well-known fact that over one thousand years ago this solitary peak was the home of a busy and devout life. This was the St. Michael's Mount of Ireland, and its history is dim and shadowy in the very early ages of Church history. Many remains of early architecture, and some of them in wonderful preservation, are still to be seen upon the summit of the rock, and form the chief magnet which draws the traveller hither.

As one begins to grow more familiar with the scene, and to lose something of the awe which it at first inspires, one cannot but feel that a true instinct brought hither the monks in those far-off days. Starting from the lighthouse, the ascent is very fine. 'Above, the rock towers higher and higher, and is split into fantastic forms like the opened leaves of a book set upright, with narrow strips of bright green running between them, or fringing the horizontal blocks of the strata at their feet. When the sunlit mists or vapours sweep in driving clouds above them, the effect is in the highest degree mysterious and beautiful; but when at one moment these mists rise so as entirely to conceal the heights, and at the next they vanish as if at the touch of some unseen hand, and the cliff again stands revealed against the blue unfathomed sky, it seems as if the whole scene were called up by some strange magician's wand.

'The ancient approach to the monastery from the landing-place was on the north-east side. There are 620 steps from a point of the cliff which is about 120 feet above the level of the sea, up to the monastery. The rest of this flight of steps is broken away, and a new approach was cut in very recent times. The old stairs run in a varying line; the steps, which grow broader towards the upper half of the ascent, are lined with tufts and long cushions of the sea-pink, and at each turn the ocean is seen breaking in foam hundreds of feet below.'[1]

For many centuries the island has been the scene of pilgrimage, but

[1] Dunraven's *Notes on Irish Architecture,* pp. 27, 28.

the author could get no certain information as to when the practice ceased, if it has come to an end. Half way up the ascent is a little valley between the two peaks, in shape something like a saddle, and known as 'Christ's Saddle,' or the Garden of the Passion. From this place what is known as the Way of the Cross rises up, and at one part a rock has been shaped into the form of a rude cross. The path still rises, and at length brings the climber to the Cashel or enclosing wall of the monastery. And a wonderful spot this is. Around is the sky and sea. In the far distance is the outline of the Irish coast, but a most peculiar effect is produced upon the mind and spirit by the physical properties of the spot. One cannot at first shake off the sense of insecurity ; then the loneliness of a high elevation oppresses one ; and yet the disturbing influence of these feelings is soothed by the consciousness that the spot is rich in its spiritual helpfulness. It is good for the soul to be thus lifted out of and away from all the mean and petty detail of life, to escape from the wearing friction of the selfish every-day life, and to be alone with the noblest natural features

THE ANCIENT STAIRCASE ON THE GREAT SKELLIG, SHOWING THE LESSER SKELLIG IN THE DISTANCE.

(From an autotype in Lord Dunraven's *Notes on Irish Architecture.*)

—the wide sky, the broad and health-giving ocean, the immovable rock, so firmly rooted that through countless generations the Atlantic surges have vainly thundered against it. Standing there one feels that when other countless generations shall have passed the rock will abide there still.

Another element in this potent charm is the conviction that upon this rock the men of the past met, and fought, and conquered those foes with which the true spirit of man is ever at war. We might not be able to use the

K 2

forms of prayer through which those men expressed their penitence, their praise, their aspiration. We may differ altogether from their conception of life, and think that they were better placed when on the mainland, and nearer the full tide of their brethren's life, and toils, and conflicts and temptations. But few can stand on that lonely elevation, bound up indissolubly as it is with so much that is sublime in the present, and hallowed in the past, without feeling lifted, for a time at least, out of the low commonplace, and the mean selfishness of too much of our daily life.

The spirit recognises that here in past ages men sought the great Father in heaven, and found that God is love; here, they yearned for pardon and found the true 'way of the cross,' the forgiveness of sins made possible because Jesus Christ died on the cross, and granted to erring man, for the Father, having given the Son, with Him freely gave them all things. These rude, humble stone cells become radiant as one feels that in them answers to prayer were obtained, and that in them men, our brothers, felt the power of the Spirit of God to cleanse, to inspire, to recreate, and to exalt. And this feeling deepens as one remembers the comparative purity of that early Irish Church, which has impressed upon the world's history such personalities as Patrick, Columbkille and Columbanus. Seen under the influence of such associations, one feels the truth of these words: 'The scene is one so solemn and so sad that none should enter here but the pilgrim and the penitent. The sense of solitude, the vast heaven above, and the sublime monotonous motion of the sea beneath, would but oppress the spirit, were not that spirit brought into harmony with all that is most sacred and grand in Nature, by the depth and even by the bitterness of its own experience.'[1]

In order to give the reader a notion of what one of these early Irish monasteries was like, the accompanying plan has been engraved. To render it quite clear, a brief explanation is needful. The buildings which form this monastery occupy a piece of ground measuring about 180 feet in length by from 80 to 100 feet in width. They are, first—the Church of St. Michael, two small oratories, Nos. 5 and 7 in ground plan, and six anchorite cells or dwelling-houses. There are also two wells and five *leachta*, or places of entombment, and several rude crosses. This group of buildings was enclosed on one side by the rock, against which they were partly built, and then by the Cashel, which ran along the edge of the precipice. The old entrance was at A (see ground plan). It consisted of a flight of steps through a door, which has long been stopped up. It leads into a small level piece of ground, called the Monk's Garden, at B, then by another flight to the doorway, D, which is also closed.

St. Michael's Church (marked chapel in plan) is not the original church of the monastery, but a later structure. It is peculiar, inasmuch as it faces

[1] Dunraven's *Notes on Irish Architecture*, vol. i., p. 30.

the north-east; and its walls, now only a mass of ruins, were, but a few years since, nearly perfect. More interesting are the old cells, of which the

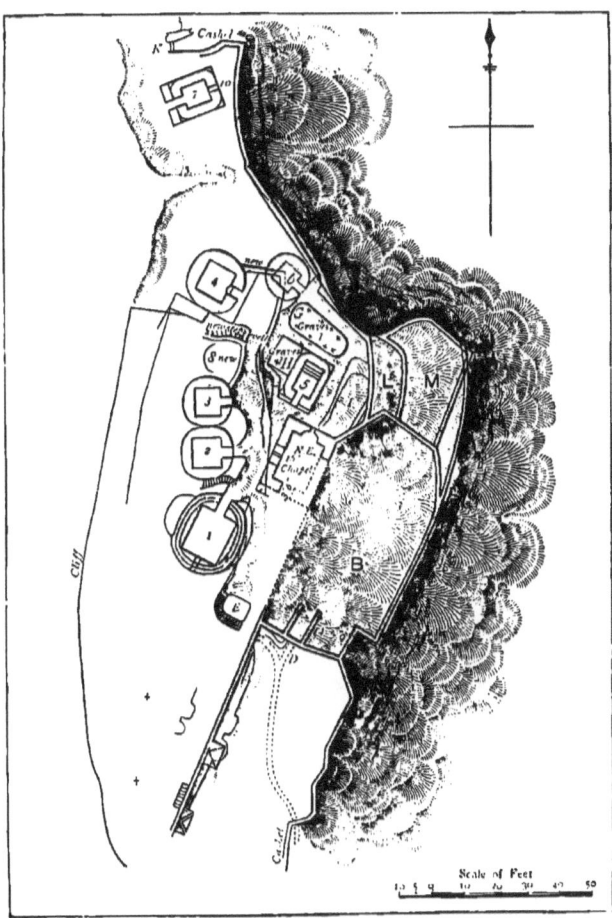

PLAN OF THE MONASTERY ON THE GREAT SKELLIG.

(From Dunraven's *Notes on Irish Architecture.*)

Cashel contains several fine specimens. No. 1 is a circular structure having what is known as a bee-hive roof. Each stone projects on the inside a little beyond the one beneath, and gradually in this way the roof comes to a point closed by a single stone. These erections belong to a very ancient period of early Irish ecclesiastical architecture. The interior is 16 feet 6 inches high, and the walls are 6 feet thick. No. 2 is rectangular inside, better built than No. 1, and composed of larger stones, some of which are dressed. Nos. 3 and 4 are similar structures. No. 5 was an oratory, and is quadrangular up to the height of 8 feet, and then becomes an oval dome. The wall at the door is 4 feet 8 inches thick. No. 6 is a cell, having on the inside 'two rows of projecting stones or pegs, which here, as also in the other cells, may have been the supports of book-satchels.' No. 7 is an oratory, stands alone, and gives evidence of being the oldest of the whole group of buildings by reason of the very rude nature of the building. No. 8, for a similar reason, is supposed to be the oldest of the cells. It is partly hidden by a wall built up against it in modern times.

G. H. are old burial-grounds, containing many rude crosses and pillar stones.

Our knowledge of the history of the Great Skellig is neither full nor consecutive, but there are very interesting references to it in the chief Irish writers. Keating[1] tells the story of how in ancient days the Milesians were wrecked off the south-west coast of Ireland by the powerful enchantments of the Tuatha de Danaans, and goes on to relate that 'the valiant Ir, the son of Milesius, with his ship, met the same fate ; for he was divided from the fleet, and was driven upon the western coast of Desmond, in the kingdom of Ireland, where he split upon the rocks, and every man perished. The body of this unfortunate prince was cast upon the shore, and was buried in a small island called Sceilig Mhichil. This place, by reason of its peculiar qualities, deserves a particular description. It is a kind of rock, situated a few leagues in the sea, and since St. Patrick's time much frequented by way of piety and devotion ; the top of it is flat and plain, and though the depth of earth be but shallow, it is observed to be of a very fattening nature, and feeds abundance of wild fowl that are forced to be confined upon it ; I say they are forced, because the surface of the ground, it is supposed, has that attractive virtue as to draw down all the birds that attempt to fly over it, and oblige them to alight upon the rock. The people who live nigh resort hither in small boats, when the sea is calm, to catch these birds, whose flesh being very sweet they use for provision, and their feathers for other occasions ; and it is to be observed that these fowl, though almost innumerable, are exceeding fat, notwithstanding the top of the rock is but small, and does not exceed three acres of land. The isle is surrounded by high and almost inaccessible precipices that hang dreadfully over the sea, which is generally rough, and roars hideously beneath. There is but one track, and that very narrow, that leads up to the top, and the ascent is so difficult and frightful that few are so hardy as to attempt it.'

[1] General History of Ireland (1854 edition, crown 8vo), p. 136.

Although Keating states that since St. Patrick's day the rock has been a place of pilgrimage, there is no historical evidence of this fact. The Annals record several plunderings of the islet by the Danes about 823 A.D. For example, under that date the Annals of Ulster state, 'Eitgau of Scelig was carried away by the strangers, and soon died of hunger and thirst.'

Giraldus Cambrensis, in his *Topographia Hiberniae*, a work dating from A.D. 1187, thus refers to the Skelligs: 'In the southern part of Munster, in the neighbourhood of Cork, there is an island with a church dedicated to St. Michael, famed for its orthodox sanctity from very ancient times;' and Lord Dunraven[1] gives a passage from an ancient MS., extracted by Mr. W. M. Hennesy, to the following effect: 'This Rocke stands three leagues from the earth in the main ocean. Itt is all at lest 700 perches long or heigh, and with much adoe one man can climb up the stayres to it at a tyme, if he looks of any side he will be afrayd of falling into sea. Att the top of this rock is a church built, and a churchyeard about it, people coming too for to perform a pilgrimage on that Rocke. There is a fount or well springing out of the Rocke in the top, and which is very admirable. There is no bird that threds in the said churchyeard above, but must go to the very brinke or bancke thereof afore they can fly; they can fly over it, but if they light in that place they can never fly until they run to the brink as afforesaide. It is named from the Archangell St. Michaell, in Irish Sceilig Mhichil.'

We are not bound in this later age to accept as undoubted all the marvels attributed to the Rock in ancient times, but these references show that in remote days, no less than now, it was difficult of approach, and that its religious associations stirred some of the deepest emotions of the heart.

But the afternoon is wearing on, the wind is freshening a little, and though we would gladly linger for hours, prudence warns us that it is time to depart. A large proportion of the population of the island accompanies us to the cove, where our boat is tossing somewhat restlessly upon waters that are in much more lively motion than when we landed. The tide is high, and the boatmen's care and skill are enlisted in the task of getting us safely embarked. Any nervous hesitation, or a foot slipping at the critical moment, might now be serious, for the boat is rising from four to six feet as each surge of the tide rolls into the cove. But in a few moments we are all safely on board, and the bow pointing towards Port Magee. We are not one hundred yards from the island before we have clear evidence that the sea is higher and the breeze stronger than it was two hours before. The white caps of the breaking waves are here and there to be seen, and though the four rowers put their strength into each pull, we seem to leave the Great Skellig only very slowly behind us. And again and again does the eye delight in its almost savage and yet fascinating

[1] *Notes on Irish Architecture*, vol. i., p. 36.

outlines. For a time the weather seems inclined to give us a touch of one of its rougher moods. As it is, we have to shape our course so as to run to the south of Puffin Island, so called because frequented by puffins. And after a really hard pull of an hour and a half's duration, we get under its lee, and the work gets easier. The row northwards, almost immediately under the frowning cliffs of the mainland, enables us to study closely the splendid peculiarities of this coast ; and the nearer inspection only deepens the first impression, viz., that it is a cruel coast for any boat or ship in distress, but that it is a superb coast for the magnificent way in which it seems to assert its permanent supremacy to the restless, passionate, and eagerly on-rushing ocean.

As we enter the harbour, and glide into the still water, the surf in the outer ledges and reefs thundering more loudly and heavily than in the morning, the sun again shines forth. We take a long, lingering farewell of the sapphire islets, and enjoy a lovely evening walk home through the heart of Valentia from Port Magee to the hotel at Knights Town, having added another to the too short list of our notable days of travel and adventure.

A STONE ORATORY AT SALLERUS, COUNTY KERRY.

AT CASTLE CONNELL ON THE SHANNON.
(From a sketch by Charles Whymper.)

ATHLONE CASTLE.

(From a photograph by Lawrence, of Dublin.)

CHAPTER VI.

THE SHANNON.

IRELAND is exceedingly rich in rivers and loughs. The traveller marvels, first, at the extent and beauty of these natural high-roads, and, secondly, at the comparatively slight use made of them for traffic and commerce. In Queenstown Harbour, near the port of Moville, in Lough Foyle, in Belfast Lough, and in Dublin Harbour, there are signs of a busy shipping trade. But even these splendid harbours do not impress the observer as being in any degree embarrassed by its quantity. And, on the other hand, such arms of the sea as Carlingford Lough, Donegal Bay, Galway Bay, and, above all, the estuary of the Shannon—waterways which many a land would be only too glad to possess and to utilise —are nearly devoid of shipping. The sail from Limerick to Kilrush fills the visitor with amazement. He rejoices in the size of this Irish Mississippi, and in the fine old ruined castles, and the lovely views to be seen along the banks. But while the steamer glides down the stream hour after hour, and few, if any, vessels pass it on their upward way, he is led to marvel how and why it comes to pass that such a superb channel is so conspicuously deserted. Nature has enriched no other European countries with such magnificent waterways, only to see them comparatively unused.

Ireland also compares favourably with England in her rivers. England can well hold her own in scenery; but it is doubtful whether she can show river country equal in beauty to the Avonmore, the Blackwater, the Barrow, the Suir, the Nore, the Boyne and its branches. However this may be it is certain that no river in England equals the Shannon, either as an estuary, or in extent, or in the interest attaching to the towns and districts along its course. We propose in this chapter to trace the course of the great stream from the source to the ocean, visiting the more famous places and districts as we pass.

The Shannon is 240 miles long, and it drains 4,544 square miles of country. It is navigable for large vessels as far as Limerick, that is, some sixty miles up from the mouth, and the greater part of its course, a total distance of 234 miles,

THE HOUSE IN WHICH MARIA EDGEWORTH LIVED.

is available for small vessels. The source, according to the popular account, is a limestone cauldron, known as 'The Shannon Pot,' situated in a mountain valley in Cavan, having on the west the Lurganacallagh Mountain, and on the east Cuilcagh Mountain. But Professor Hull asserts that experiment has proved the real source to be 'a little lough, situated about a mile from the Shannon Pot, which receives considerable drainage from the ground surrounding it at the base of Tiltibane, but has no visible outlet. The waters from the little lough flow in a subterranean channel till they issue forth at the so-called source of the Shannon.' The river flowing in a southerly course is reinforced by the Owenmore River, a considerable stream with several affluents which drains the valley between Cuilcagh and Slievenakula Mountains, and which has itself a fair claim to be considered the real headwaters of the Shannon. The combined streams soon leave Cavan and flow through Leitrim, broadening out into Lough Allen, the first of a series of fine sheets of water along the course of the river.

In its southerly course the stream passes by Carrick-on-Shannon, Jamestown, Loughs Baderg and Forbes, and forms the boundary between Connaught and Leinster, separating Roscommon on the west from Longford and West Meath on the east. About nine miles from the town of Longford is a spot famous in the literary history not only of Ireland, but also of the United Kingdom. In 1583, a family named Edgeworth established itself at the village called Edgeworthstown, the head of it at that date being Bishop of Down and Connor. The family has always held a high place among those who felt it a duty to labour for the benefit and social improvement of those around them.

During the last century, Richard Edgeworth did much to improve the estate, and was a noted landlord, but it is to the pen of his daughter that the wide reputation of the family is due, and the *Moral Tales* have been read wherever English is known. The house in which the Edgeworths have resided for generations is a plain, comfortable mansion, and in

THE LIBRARY IN WHICH MARIA EDGEWORTH WROTE.

this house, which is still standing, the stories were written which have delighted and benefited thousands of readers.

Dr. Macaulay, in the *Leisure Hour* for 1873, thus describes the place to which he then journeyed as a literary pilgrim: 'Edgeworthstown is not a show place, nor is it to be seen without special permission. Having obtained this, I spent some pleasant hours there. Yet it was a melancholy kind of pleasure, the silent and deserted rooms peopling themselves with the shadows of the generation now all but passed away. Maria Edgeworth died in 1850, yet the library or study where she wrote most of the works which have made her name world-famous is just as she left it. It is a large, low-roofed room, with thick projecting wood pillars and wainscoting, and with cosy recesses. Her writing-table and chair, and old family bits of furniture are still there. The walls are covered with pictures, chiefly family portraits, of which there are also several in the fine entrance hall. All parts of the house are full of interesting family records and relics.'

Maria Edgeworth's father was married four times, and had no less than twenty-two children. She was the eldest, and in 1814 she wrote: 'His eldest child was above five-and-forty, the youngest being only one year old.' It was the responsibility thus thrust upon her, combined with natural aptitude for the work, which enabled her to practise in that large family the precepts she embodied in her numerous writings.

Between Longford and Athlone the Shannon widens out into Lough Ree, a picturesque lake, possessing the broken outline common to loughs formed by the chemical solution of limestone rocks. The banks are well wooded, and the surface of the lake is broken by islands, some of which are exceedingly beautiful. Not very far from the southern end of Lough Ree is the village of Lissory or Auburn, which claims to be the birthplace of Oliver Goldsmith, and which certainly was the scene of his early childhood and youth. He was born at Pallas, in County Longford, in November, 1728, and when the boy was only a few years old, his father, a curate, was presented with the living of Auburn, where he was not simply 'passing rich on forty pounds a year,' after the standard of *The Deserted Village*, but in fairly comfortable circumstances, for the living was worth about £200 a year. As a boy Oliver Goldsmith had a hard life. He was not attractive in appearance, and the smallpox left most evident traces upon his countenance of the severity with which it had visited him. From Auburn, when he was sixteen, he went up as a sizar to Trinity College, Dublin, and while there he so failed to utilise his time and opportunities that neither the keenest insight nor the liveliest imagination could have predicted that the day would come when the institution in which he had been caned by a tutor would erect, on one of the most prominent sites in the Irish metropolis, a statue to his memory. Goldsmith was a poet and a man of letters, and it has long been recognised that literary men of genius seldom develop in accordance with fixed rule, or in orderly response to academic training.

It has often been supposed that in Goldsmith's famous poem, *The Deserted Village*, which appeared in 1770, he has sketched Auburn. Lord Macaulay's criticism is probably just: 'It is made up of two incongruous parts. The village in its happy days is a true English village; the village in its decay is an Irish village. He had assuredly never seen in his native island such a rural paradise, such a seat of plenty, content, and tranquillity, as his Auburn. He had assuredly never seen in England all the inhabitants of such a paradise turned out of their homes in one day, and forced to emigrate in a body to America. The hamlet he had probably seen in Kent; the ejectment he had probably seen in Munster; but, by joining the two, he has produced something which never was and never will be seen in any part of the world.'

Two miles below Lough Ree the Shannon flows past Athlone, one of the most important and noted of Irish inland towns. It is a busy market

OLIVER GOLDSMITH.

town, a great military centre, possessing also a valuable salmon fishery. The main line of rail between Dublin and Galway here crosses the Shannon by a handsome 'bowstring and lattice' iron swivel bridge. This is 560 feet long, has four spans, two of 175 feet each over the river, and two of 40 feet each, over a road on each bank. The castle is supposed to date from King John's time, and is still well kept up, being an important and imposing structure. Adjoining it are barracks capable of accommodating a small army. Athlone was the scene of stirring adventures in 1641, and in 1691 it was besieged and captured by General Ginkell. The bulk of the town lies opposite the castle, and on the left bank of the Shannon. The famous old bridge, the scene of many a conflict, was taken down some years ago, and replaced by the handsome and convenient structure depicted in the engraving. Athlone is not well built, nor does it contain much that need delay the visitor. But there is an air of bustle and prosperity about it that presents a pleasing contrast with some not very distant neighbours.

Athlone is the most convenient starting-point for an excursion that should rank among the most important in Ireland, viz., a visit to Clonmacnois. At one time steamers plied down the Shannon from Athlone to Killaloe ; but at the time of writing (1888) this is not the case. A steamer may occasionally go, but this happens too seldom to be of much service to strangers. This is a misfortune, for the trip is one of the best in Ireland. But to visit Clonmacnois the visitor can either hire a row boat and pull down the river, or go by road in a car, a distance of nearly twelve miles. By the latter method he sees to advantage a fine stretch of country, and enjoys some strong fresh air. The district is undulating, and the road winds along past country houses, through tiny hamlets, by deserted cabins, and over large stretches of bog, giving every here and there fine views over the Shannon Valley, and at last brings the visitor to the far-famed ' Meadow of the Son of Nos,' this being the real meaning of the name Clonmacnois.

This famous ecclesiastical establishment is well situated upon a knoll overlooking a wide sweep and curve of the Shannon. Within a Cashel, or stone enclosure, are some magnificent architectural remains, and upon another knoll, only a stone's throw distant, are traces of the ancient structure which served as the episcopal palace and castle of the O'Melaghlins. Clonmacnois was founded in A.D. 546 by St. Kieran on land given by Dermot MacCervail, King of Ireland. It soon became a city, and the seat of a bishopric, and established a great reputation as a seat of learning. In later times it became a favourite cemetery for kings and nobles. It was ravaged again and again by the Northmen, and the centuries have not treated it very kindly. But notwithstanding these vicissitudes, and the destructive influences that have been exerted upon it, it is yet second to no spot in Ireland for the number and interest of its wonderful remains.

These consist of churches, round towers, stone crosses, and ancient tombs. The building known as Temple Conor is now used as a parish church. This church dates from the tenth century, but of the original edifice, in all probability, the doorway, of which we give an illustration, is the only part extant. The Daimhliag Mor, or Great Church, was built in 909 by Flann, King of Ireland, and Colman, Abbot of Clonmacnois. It was rebuilt in the fourteenth century; but the splendid west doorway is in all probability a part of the original structure. The north doorway, which is enriched by three sculptures placed above the arch—St. Patrick in his pontificals, with St. Francis on one side and St. Dominic on the other—is of the later date. Standing within the church and looking out through the western door, the visitor sees one of the finest ancient crosses in Ireland. It has evidently been placed there purposely, and, seen through the frame of a doorway that was two centuries old when Henry II. landed in Ireland, standing out boldly and clearly as it does against the distant

sky, this great, time-worn cross deeply impresses the imagination. About its origin there is no doubt. Upon the west side is the inscription, 'A prayer for Flann, son of Maelsechlainn,' and upon the eastern, 'A prayer for Colman who made this cross on the King Flann.' King Flann died in A.D. 916, and Abbot Colman in 924 or 926, and this magnificent monument, 15 feet high, and so placed that no worshipper could leave the church without seeing it, has for over nine hundred years testified to the piety of the monarch, and to the skill of the men by whom he was served and remembered. On the side of the cross facing the church are sculptures relating to the original foundation of that edifice by St. Kieran, who is represented with a hammer in one hand and a mallet in the other. The

DOORWAY OF TEMPLE CONOR CHURCH, CLONMACNOIS.

other side has carvings depicting scenes in our Lord's Passion. A short distance to the south stands another large cross, nearly as fine a specimen of this kind of art as Flann's. It is a good example of the embossed ornamentation common in Irish sculpture of this period. The engraving on page 146 represents this in the foreground, with Flann's cross and the big Round Tower in the middle, and the Shannon in the distance. The numerous tombstones, ancient and modern, testify to the sanctity of Clonmacnois.

There are two Round Towers. That shown in the engraving, although ruined in the upper portion, is one of the largest and finest in the country. It is contemporary, in all probability, with Flann's Church. Cæsar Otway's

L

description of it is not only appropriate to this, but applies to many other specimens of this characteristic Irish building. 'It was high enough,' he writes, 'to take cognisance of the coming enemy, let him come from what point he might; it commanded the ancient causeway that was laid down at considerable expense across the great bog on the Connaught side

THE LARGE ROUND TOWER AND THE CROSSES AT CLONMACNOIS.
(From a photograph by Lawrence, of Dublin.)

of the Shannon; it looked up and down the river, and commanded the tortuous and sweeping reaches of the stream, as it unfolded itself like an uncoiling serpent along the surrounding bogs and marshes; it could hold communication with the holy places of Clonfert; and from the top of its pillared height send its beacon light towards the sacred isles and anchorite retreats of Lough Ree; it was large and roomy enough to contain all the officiating priests of Clonmacnois, with their pyxes, vestments, and books; and though the Pagan Dane or wild Munsterman might rush on in rapid inroad, yet the solitary watcher on the tower was ready to give warning, and collect within the protecting pillar all holy men and things, until the tyranny was overpast.'

This extract admirably describes the most important functions of these curious buildings. No point in Irish archæology has been more controverted than the origin and use of the Round Towers. Dr. Petrie has, in the opinion of most scholars, settled the question once for all in his well-known essay. They were watch-towers from which the approach of an enemy might be descried in time to make adequate preparations for defence. They were secure places of refuge, into which the monks and all connected with the monastery could safely retire with their valuables, when they were unable otherwise to withstand the assaults of the Northmen. They were also belfrys or bell-towers, and this may be described as their normal use. In them hung the bell or bells that summoned the various members of the monastery to their duties, and that announced the various services as they were held.

During five or six hundred years the great tower of Clonmacnois discharged these varied functions. It was built, in Dr. Petrie's view, about A.D. 908. In the *Annals of the Four Masters*, under A.D. 1124, we read : 'The finishing of the *cloictheach* (the Irish term used to describe these towers, and meaning belfry) of Clonmacnois by O'Malone, successor of St. Kieran.' This entry referred in all probability not to the erection but to a restoration of the tower. And as late as 1552, in the same Annals, the following entry appears : 'Clonmacnois was plundered and devastated by the Galls (English) of Athlone, and the large bells were carried from the *cloictheach*. There was not left, moreover, a bell, small or large, an image, or an altar, or a book, or a gem, or even glass in a window, from the wall of the church out, which was not carried off. Lamentable was this deed, the plundering of the city of Ciaran, the holy patron.'

Over a hundred specimens of these buildings, some of them quite perfect, have survived to this day. They resemble each other in plan and construction, some exhibiting better masonry than others, and local peculiarities in some instances determining the position of the windows and the door. Usually this is found, as shown in the engraving on page 146, about 15 feet from the ground. This fact strengthens the view that one main purpose the towers served was to afford a safe refuge. When the defenders had entered, and the ladder by which they ascended was removed, they were practically unassailable by any weapons the Northmen possessed. These doors were sometimes decorated with ornamental carvings, but more generally consisted of simple arches.

The second tower at Clonmacnois belongs to the building known as

Teampul Finghin, or Fineen's Church, dating, it is supposed, from the tenth century, of which only the chancel and round tower remain. In this instance the tower is perfect.   It is much smaller than its companion, being only fifty-six feet high, and the doorway is on a level with the floor of the chancel and opens into it.

Many interesting tombstones exist at Clonmacnois, and many interesting objects of antiquity have been found there.   Among these the museum of the Royal Irish Academy in Dublin possesses a crozier which once belonged to the bishops of Clonmacnois, and which is a very fine specimen of this kind of Irish art.

But here, as at Glendalough, although a minute acquaintance with the history and archæology adds greatly to the value and educational

DOORWAY OF THE LARGER ROUND TOWER AT CLONMACNOIS.

value of a visit, the absence of these by no means destroys the interest of Clonmacnois.   The situation is very lovely, the view of the Shannon very fine, the ride or the row from Athlone enjoyable, and even the most superficial inspection of the towers and arches and ruined churches can hardly fail to enrich the visitor with new and deep impressions of the vigorous religious life of Ireland eight hundred or a thousand years ago.

Leaving Clonmacnois and following the course of the great river, Shannonbridge and Banaghel are passed, and finally we reach Portumna.   Here a swivel bridge, 766 feet long, has replaced an earlier wooden structure built by Lemuel Cox, the architect of the still extant Waterford Bridge.   There is nothing of special interest in Portumna, but the district around has become notorious in recent years on account of its agrarian troubles.   Into these, however, it is not our function to enter.

A few miles to the east of Portumna is Birr or Parsonstown, the residence of the late Earl Rosse, whose achievements in connection with the telescope are well known.   Birr Castle is a fine pile of buildings, some portions of which are very ancient.   About 1610 it came into the possession of the present family by a grant on the part of James I. to Sir Lawrence Parsons.   The great telescopes were built by the father of the present earl some fifty years ago.   They are three in number, and are all reflectors ; one 18 inches in diameter, one 3 feet in diameter, and the Great Telescope, six feet in diameter and 60 feet long, the largest astronomical instrument in the world. It was first erected in 1842, and although some improvements have been made in the mounting, these are not very important. The concave mirrors are metal in all three, that of the Leviathan weighing nearly four tons. By the aid of these splendid instruments the late and the present earls have added greatly to our knowledge of the nebulæ and of some branches of astronomical physics.

Below Portumna the river widens out into Lough Derg, about 25 miles long, with an average width of from 2 to 3 miles. The scenery along the whole of the lake is very fine, especially at Scariff Bay. From Mount Shannon on the north shore of the bay, Iniscalthra, one of the many Holy Islands of Ireland, should be visited. St. Caiman founded a monastery here in the seventh century. The church he built was restored by Brian Boru, and of this building considerable ruins are still extant. There is also a fine round tower, partly ruined, but still 80 feet high. At the southern end of Lough Derg is the town of Killaloe, once the seat of power of King Brian Boru. The situation of the town is most picturesque, and it is rich in the possession of a very ancient church. An abbey was founded here in the sixth century by St. Molua, and on its site now stands the cathedral, which dates from the end of the twelfth century. Hard by the cathedral is a small stone-roofed church, which Dr. Petrie believes may be referred to St. Flannan, Molua's disciple, who was consecrated Bishop of Killaloe about A.D. 639. On a beautiful wooded island in the river stand the ruined nave and choir of a stone-roofed church belonging to the oldest buildings of the class in Western Europe, and considered by Dr. Petrie to be a church originally built by St. Molua. In these days the island is frequented by anglers, amongst whom it holds a high character, as affording ample facilities for their sport.

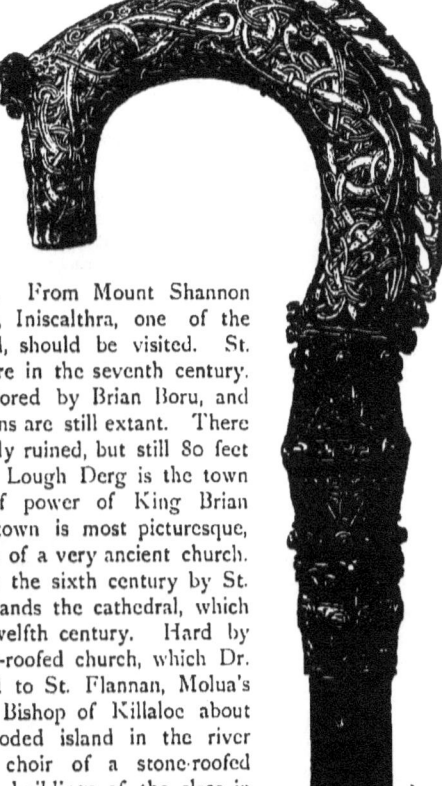

CROZIER FOUND AT CLONMACNOIS.

At Killaloe, and between that town and Limerick, the course of the Shannon is broken by rapids, and consequently the water traffic between those two places is carried on by canal. About midway between the two

towns is one of the loveliest bits of landscape in Ireland. This place is
known as Castle Connell, and here occur what are generally called the Falls
of Doonass. The waters of the Shannon, which are here in some places
40 feet deep and 300 yards wide, for a distance of half a mile rush and roar
over ledges of rock and huge boulders. The effect of the scene, which is
really very impressive, is due not to anything like a high fall. It owes its
charm to the fact that the Shannon makes a wide curve, the banks are
either precipitous and well-wooded, or else bordered by fine and well-kept
demesnes, and rushing along between the beautiful banks is the noble
stream, its surface broken up into falls and whirlpools and hurrying rapids;
the ever-changing and yet ever-constant forms delighting the eye, and the
varied tones of the troubled waters combining into a volume of sound
delightful and refreshing to the ear. Few spots are better suited for a
quiet walk, for a summer picnic, and, above all, for the pursuit of Izaak
Walton's craft. Even a short walk along the river can seldom be taken
at this point during the season without the sight of a salmon or a trout
capture. Nor is this operation limited to its legitimate pursuit. Walking
along the right bank of the stream, sheltered corners are shown in the
rocks where fires can be lit to attract the salmon, and report has it that
poaching after this fashion is by no means uncommon.

Soon after leaving Castle Connell, Limerick is reached, by far the most
important city on the Shannon, one of the important centres of trade in
Ireland, and a place that has been prominent in some of the most stirring
episodes in history. It was founded by the Danes in the ninth century.
From them it passed under the sway of the family of Brian Boru, thus
attaining to the dignity of the royal city of Munster. It then fell into
the hands of the Thomond kings, who ruled it during the twelfth century.
King John erected a strong castle there; it was often besieged in the
thirteenth and fourteenth centuries. Elizabeth made it a centre of adminis-
tration; Ireton captured it in 1651; in the Stuart struggle it held with
James II., and having been unsuccessfully assaulted by William III. in
1690, in 1691 it capitulated under the treaty which led to a series of events
the memory of which has given Limerick the name of the 'City of the
Violated Treaty.'

Limerick is finely situated upon both banks of the Shannon and upon
King's Island, which is formed by the Abbey River. It is divided into three
main districts; English Town, which occupies the island, Irish Town, which
lies to the south of the island—these two constituting the 'Old Town'—
and Newtown Pery, the chief business and residential districts of to-day.
From the peculiarities of its situation, Limerick is rich in bridges. Three
cross the Shannon, two of them being handsome structures. One, the
Athlunkard Bridge, is hardly within the town. It crosses a beautiful
reach of the river above the city, and carries the Killaloe Road. The

Wellesley Bridge, connecting Newtown Pery with the road from Ennis, is a fine specimen of modern engineering, and consists of five arches, with a swivel on the city side. Higher up the river is Thomond Bridge, rebuilt in 1839, which stands on the site of the ancient bridge, and was the scene of many important events in the past history of the city. Few towns in the United Kingdom can exhibit such large structures so finely placed as these two bridges.

At the western end of Thomond Bridge, raised upon a substantial pedestal which lifts it above the reach of the chipping tourist or the wanton defacer, stands the stone upon which, according to popular belief, the Treaty of Limerick was signed in 1691. The history of this famous

THOMOND BRIDGE, LIMERICK.

negotiation is long and complex. One of the articles stipulated that the Roman Catholics should enjoy the same privileges in the exercise of their religion as they had done in the reign of Charles II., and that they were to be protected from religious persecution. This article does not seem to have been kept, and hence the name so frequently applied to Limerick— the 'City of the Violated Treaty.'

Thomond Bridge gains in picturesque beauty from the fact that at the eastern end stands King John's Castle. This has been greatly disfigured by the construction of unsightly barracks within its precincts; but these have not been able to wholly destroy the fine effect of the old turrets and towers rising above the bold arches of the bridge, as seen from the opposite bank of the Shannon. Frowning down upon the main approach to English Town,

the massive gateway and the drum towers tell the tale of force and con-
quest invariably associated here and elsewhere with the traces of the
Norman and Anglo-Norman times.   The only other building likely to
interest the visitor stands in English Town.   This is Limerick Cathedral ;
it differs from many churches in departing from the crucifix form, and
consists of three aisles.   It is considered to date from the twelfth century,

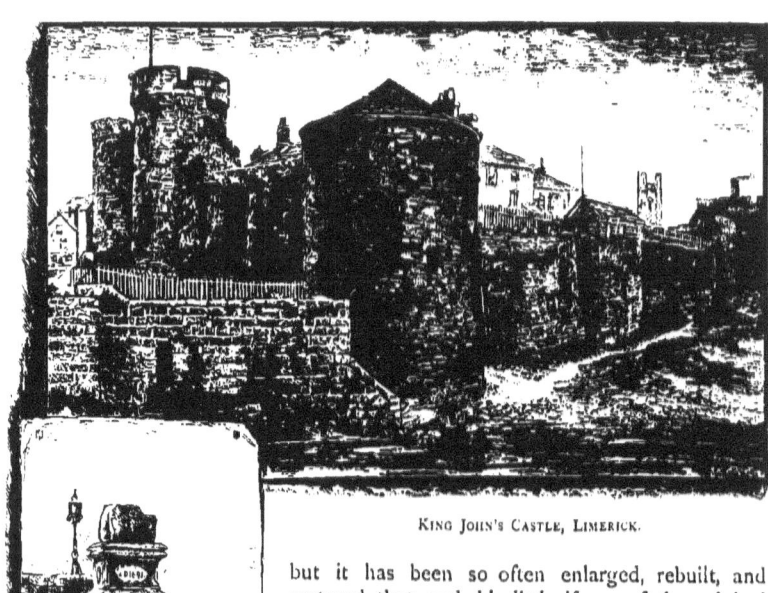

KING JOHN'S CASTLE, LIMERICK.

THE TREATY STONE, LIMERICK.

but it has been so often enlarged, rebuilt, and
restored that probably little if any of the original
edifice remains.   The interior is effective, and
there are many tombs in it, some of considerable
interest and merit ; the two side aisles are divided
into chapels.   There is a splendid tower at the
west end, and from the top a view of this part
of the Shannon valley is obtained which no visitor
who wishes to appreciate the beauty of the
Limerick suburbs should miss.   At his feet lies the city, intersected by the
rivers, and the eye can easily follow the windings of the cramped streets that
occupy the older parts.   Away on every side stretches a fine expanse of
country.   Looking up the Shannon, the stream can be traced a considerable
part of the way towards Castle Connell and Lough Derg, while below the
city it can be seen hastening on to the noble estuary.   On every side the

view is beautifully framed in by the near or distant hills which enclose one
of the most fertile districts of Ireland.

The tower contains a peal of bells noted for their sweetness of tone, and
concerning which the following legend is related :—'The founder of the bells,
an Italian, having wandered through many lands, at last, after the lapse of
long years, arrived in the Shannon one summer evening. As he sailed up
the river, he started at hearing his long lost bells ring out a glorious chime ;
with intensified attention he listened to their tones, and when his companions
tried to arouse him from his ecstasy they found he had died of joy.'

From this point of vantage a fair appreciation of the most brilliant
exploit performed by Limerick's military hero, Sarsfield, may be obtained.
When, in 1690, William III. was marching upon Limerick, expecting an easy
capture, it was only by Sarsfield's energy and courage that the resolution
was taken to resist to the last. Things looked gloomy indeed for the Irish
cause. William and his army arrived and pitched their tents ; at some
distance in the rear followed ammunition trains and supplies, together with
some heavy ordnance, and a bridge of ten boats. Sarsfield, with the skill of a
true soldier, saw that his one supreme hope was to destroy the enemy's train.
The incident can hardly be better described than in Lord Macaulay's words :
' A few hours, therefore, after the English tents had been pitched before
Limerick, Sarsfield set forth under cover of the night with a strong body
of horse and dragoons. He took the road to Killaloe, and crossed the
Shannon there ; during the day he lurked with his band in a wild mountain tract named from the silver mines which it contains. He learned in
the evening that the detachment which guarded the English artillery had
halted for the night seven miles from William's camp on a pleasant carpet
of green turf, and under the ruined walls of an old castle ; that officers and
men seemed to think themselves perfectly secure ; that the beasts had been
turned loose, and that even the sentinels were dozing. When it was dark
the Irish horsemen quitted their hiding-place, and were conducted by the
people of the country to the spot where the escort lay sleeping round the
guns. The surprise was complete ; some of the English sprang to their
arms, and made an attempt to resist, but in vain ; about sixty fell, one
only was taken alive. The victorious Irish made a huge pile of waggons
and pieces of cannon. Every gun was stuffed with powder, and fixed with
its mouth in the ground, and the whole mass was blown up. The solitary
prisoner, a lieutenant, was treated with great civility by Sarsfield. "If I
had failed in this attempt," said the gallant Irishman, "I should have been
off to France." '

Sarsfield returned to Limerick, William was compelled to retreat, and
it was not until the following year that Sarsfield honourably capitulated to
Ginkell, and retired with a part of his army to France. A fine statue of
the general now adorns one of the streets of the city.

Limerick has some fine streets and handsome buildings ; the former are thronged by many varieties of Irish society, and by not a few of the fair sex, whose beauty has added to the fame of the city. William Street and George Street are good thoroughfares, crowded with business houses and attractive shops. At the same time it must be admitted that Limerick, even more than many Irish centres of trade, presents those ruined and dismantled houses, even in the better-class streets, which strike the traveller's eye so curiously and unfavourably. The Roman Catholic Cathedral of St. John is a fine Gothic structure. Beyond the top of George Street is the Convent of St. Vincent, and not far away is a large and handsome church. One week evening the writer saw this building, which is capable of holding seventeen hundred people, crammed to the doors by men who had come —and whom he was informed came regularly every week—to a service in connection with the religious and temperance guild worked by the Redemptorist Fathers, to whom the church belongs. Two services are held each week, both thronged, and the guild numbers 5000 men.

Limerick has long been a centre of considerable trade, and although at the present time (1888) there is great depression in shipping, and American competition has practically destroyed Irish flour mills, nevertheless there is considerable commercial activity in the city. Lace of a very superior quality has long been produced here, also fishhooks of a fine temper. The industry that exhibits to the stranger most signs of prosperity and extent is connected with one of the staple productions of the land—the ever-present pig—and expends great energy and capital upon the speediest and best ways of converting him into bacon and hams. There is a mistaken idea current that this process can be seen to advantage only in the United States ; that is a great delusion. There are larger pig-killing establishments at Cincinnati and Chicago, doubtless, but at none of them is there a greater combination of smartness, neatness, cleanliness, and high quality of the bacon and ham than at Limerick. By the courtesy of the proprietors, the writer was enabled to go over the establishment of Messrs. Shaw and Sons. Multitudes of those pigs which are to be seen by almost every cabin door in Ireland, and which swarm at every market and fair, find their way here. The buyers, the sharpest and in some respects the most important members of the staff, are constantly securing in all parts of the country hundreds and thousands of pigs. They are not kept long in an active state. Very soon after the porker's arrival it becomes his turn to be chained by the hind leg, swung up to an iron bar, and before he has had time to utter more than two or three of his shrill protests, a sure and strong hand cuts short his life. In the course of the next few minutes he passes through a series of processes which result in his being cleansed, prepared, weighed, and deposited in the huge room where he awaits his turn to be made into bacon and hams. The rate at which this work is done can be gauged from the fact that sometimes 100 are weighed within the hour. Strange as it may sound, all these processes are done cleanly ; and by exceedingly ingenious arrangements of sliding rods it is very seldom necessary for the animal to be placed upon the shoulders of men. It is only by going over an establishment of this kind that some notion of the magnitude of the Irish bacon trade is obtained. Few, probably, think that the shaping of a ham has anything special about it, until they see the rough ham taking a neat and shapely form under knives used by skilful hands.

On leaving Limerick in the Kilrush boat, the shipping trade is seen in active operation along the quays. This, unfortunately, is not so brisk as it used to be ; but it still represents a large capital. The trip to the estuary occupies several hours, and is full of enjoyment to those fond of river scenery. The bridges, quays, castle, spires, and cathedral of Limerick soon disappear in the distance, and Carrig-O-Gunnell, the first of the many ruined castles of this district, comes into view. A few miles inland is Mungret, once a great centre of Irish learning, its abbey, now a ruin, formerly accommodating no fewer than 1500 monks ; and further inland still Adare, the lovely seat of Lord Dunraven, famous not only for Adare Manor, one of the finest houses in Ireland, but also for a wonderful group of ruins. These consist of a castle, the Trinitarian Friary (1230), the Austin Friary (1306), the Franciscan Friary (1464), and two ancient churches. The late earl was an enthusiastic lover of Irish antiquities, as his great work, *Notes on Irish Architecture*, proves ; and these ruins are carefully looked after. There is nothing of the kind more beautiful in the country.

Ruined castles are not quite so frequent along the lower valley of the Shannon as on the Rhine, nor are they quite so picturesquely situated ; but, like their more noted brethren, they speak of a time when violence was rampant, when men took what they could get by the strong right hand, and kept it only as long as they remained stronger than their turbulent neighbours. The old keeps alternate with fine modern country seats, this district now, no less than in the past, being a place of residence desired by many. Leaving Bunratty Castle, a massive ruin, on the right hand, and crossing the mouth of the Fergus, which is really a wide bay, Foynes, the terminus of the railway, is reached ; a few miles further the seat of the Knight of Glin is passed, and finally Tarbert is reached. The river at this part is exceedingly lovely. Below Tarbert the stream broadens out into a magnificent estuary, forming a splendid approach to the heart of the country. A run of eight or nine miles in a north-westerly direction brings the vessel to Kilrush. On the left, the ruined churches, the Round Tower, and the tiny hamlets of Scattery Island are in full view. But before this can be duly enjoyed the pier is reached, and any imaginative excursion into those far-distant days when St. Senan crossed to the island in a coracle very similar to those still to be seen on the beach is promptly terminated

by the discordant shouts of the car-drivers on the quay, each hailing some
old employer, or eager to secure a prey before a rival succeeds. For in
Kilrush there is little of interest, and most of those who come by the boat
have as their goal Kilkee.

This is the fashionable watering-place of the district, and although
Miltown Malbay and Lahinch are making a strong bid for favour, the
accommodation at Kilkee is still far ahead of any that can be shown by its
enterprising rivals. The drive from Kilrush is about nine miles, and not
specially interesting. This is a drawback; but few who reach the little
seaside place regret the trouble expended in getting there. The coast of
Clare is wild and rocky in the extreme. At Kilkee a pretty semicircular
bay has been formed, with good sands, and protected from the inrush of

KILKEE FROM THE COASTGUARD STATION.

(From a photograph by Lawrence, of Dublin.)

the Atlantic by as ugly a ledge of
rock as the most fastidious taste in
that class of scenery could desire.
It is in keeping with this terrible west coast that, even when a rare harbour,
as at Kilkee, does occur, it should be rendered very difficult to enter except
in fine weather. Around the bay, and especially on the southern side, the
West End, as it is called, cluster the houses occupied by visitors in the
summer, and deserted for the most part in the winter. The coast walks
are very fine, and the air is very fresh and bracing. Any who love, or
who need, the wind that blows in from the sea can here obtain it in remarkable purity. Those who enjoy a holiday more if they are accompanied by
their children, can see them sport in the sands at Kilkee with equanimity,
knowing that there they are safe, and certain to enjoy themselves.

Those who rejoice in wild fantastic rock scenery should be happy at
Kilkee. All along this coast the waves of the Atlantic in the course of ages

have washed away all the softer material from huge pillars of rock that yet defy the power of the sea, and appear to stand as sentinels along the shore. In some parts the angles are such that a slight exercise of the imagination can transform

CLIFFS NEAR KILKEE.

prominent points along the coast into giant faces looking down sardonically upon the waves breaking and roaring helplessly at their feet. On Bishop's Island is a very good example of a beehive oratory and a house, none the

CLIFFS AND NATURAL ARCH NEAR BALLY-
BUNNION.

(From a photograph by Lawrence, of Dublin.

less interesting from the fact that it can be fairly well studied from the mainland. Caves and natural arches abound both north and south of Kilkee. We give an engraving of a curious natural arch to be seen near Ballybunnion, on the south side of the Shannon estuary, opposite the ruins of Carrigaholt Castle, once the stronghold of the MacMahons. In fine weather boating enables the curious to look closely upon the weird cliff forms and the really wonderful rock faces of this coast; while in rough weather it may be some consolation to go and watch the sea at its fantastic tricks in the Puffing Hole.

BLESSING THE CLADDAGH FLEET AT THE BEGINNING OF THE FISHING SEASON.

(From a sketch by Charles Whymper.)

CLEW BAY.

CHAPTER VII

CONNEMARA

GALWAY is the proper starting-point for excursions into the splendid mountain country of Connemara; but as we closed our last chapter at Kilkee, it may be well to resume our travels from that point. The drive from Kilkee to Miltown Malbay runs near the coast, affording here and there some good views, but chiefly interesting because it traverses a fairly good agricultural district of County Clare, and enables the traveller to see for himself what kind of land the Clare peasants have to work, and what are the external appearances of one of the great centres of agrarian disturbance. The West Clare Railway is now open to Miltown Malbay, and the traveller

pressed for time can go via Ennis direct by rail to Galway. Much the more interesting route is to keep along the coast, visiting the cliffs of Moher, then striking inland to Lisdoonvarna, and crossing Galway Bay from Ballyvaughan.

There are several famous stretches of cliff scenery on the west coast of Ireland—Moher, Croghan on Achill Island, the cliffs between Ballina and Belmullet, Horn Head, and Slieve League. The last is the most picturesque, and impresses most powerfully the imagination, but the connoisseur should make a point of inspecting them all. The cliffs of Moher extend for several miles along the coast of Clare, reaching in one or two parts an altitude of from 600 to 700 feet. The best time to see them is during a westerly gale. On a clear day the view from the tower shown in the engraving is very comprehensive, extending over the Connemara Highlands northwards, and westward and southward from the Isles of Arran at the mouth of Galway Bay to Loop Head, the extreme point of the promontory forming the north shore of the Shannon estuary.

Lisdoonvarna is a spa, and those wishful to do so can there partake of either chalybeate or sulphur water, and at the same time study the habits of those who frequent the Irish Cheltenham.

But most visitors, after seeing Moher, prefer to leave these tamer beauties for the more rugged scenes of the north, and make all speed to Galway. Or, if coming from Dublin, they will take the comfortable and, for Ireland, fast express of the Midland Great Western Railway. By this route the visitor runs across the great central plain of the country, and over the extensive dreary tracts of the Bog of Allen, which at parts

PEAT CUTTING.
(From a sketch by Charles Whymper.)

extends for miles along both sides of the railway. But even here the dark brown colouring, the dead level, the evidences of peat cutting, and the accentuated monotony of the landscape, combine to interest those who see them for the first time. These peat bogs make up a very considerable

M 2

proportion of the soil of the country, occupying no less than 2,830,000 acres, and they arouse curiosity as to their origin. Since, like coal, they exhibit no marine fossils, they are not due to the action of the sea. But the evidence shows that they have been formed by mossy growths either in forests or upon the sediment deposited in hollows or fresh-water lakes. The continuous growth and decay during the lapse of ages has slowly built up the peat, which now varies from 20 to 40 feet in thickness, and which supplies over a great part of Ireland the lack of coal. The great bog district over which the railroad to Galway runs is believed to be due to the growth of peat-producing plants destroying the original oak forest, this being succeeded by firs, and these also perishing in turn.

Peat-cutting is one of the commonest and most characteristic occupations in Ireland. Our engraving illustrates the process in some parts of Connaught, though the commoner method is to cut the peat from above, the operator with the spade standing upon the portion to be cut away, and detaching the blocks vertically, not horizontally. The peat is cut into pieces much the size and shape of a brick. It is piled in the first instance loosely by the side of the trench from which it is cut. When sufficiently dried there, it is stacked, as shown by the piles in the distance, and it is then carried or carted by horses, ponies or donkeys to the place where it is to be sold or consumed. Most travellers in Ireland at some stage of their journeyings have reason to, and very readily can, assure themselves of the heat-giving qualities of peat.

Passing first Mullingar, that Mecca of anglers, then Athlone, already described, and finally Athenry, with its ruined castle, ancient gateway, and, if seen on market day, picturesque throng of Galway peasants, the train steams into the spacious Galway terminus, adjoining which is the huge hotel built in the hope that Galway would become, what it doubtless ought to be, a great port for the American trade.

The curious man may ramble about Galway, and find much to interest him at every turn. The streets are for the most part narrow, winding and irregular. The houses form a strange jumble. Side by side with substantial buildings of the most approved nineteenth century type, stand houses which carry the observer back to the sixteenth century, and if in their courtyards he were to see a group of Philip the Second's Spaniards, he could hardly be surprised. There is the same strange variety in the faces to be seen. Here, if nowhere else, the supposed typical Irishman is to be met, in tall hat and knee-breeches, with the short up-turned nose, small forehead and receding chin. Here also in the crowd follow faces that recall one after another the Dane, the Saxon, the Spaniard and the Celt. Here more, perhaps, than in most popular centres in Ireland the mixed character of the Irish people becomes evident.

There are but few buildings in the town of any special merit; Eyre

Square contains the best of the modern structures. Lynch's mansion in Abbeygate Street is a fine example of the kind of house the Spanish merchants lived in three centuries ago. St. Nicholas Church is well worth a visit ; the requirements of modern education are met by the Queen's College, a fine Gothic building, which stands on the western bank of the River Corrib, in the northern suburbs.

The town possesses a very fine harbour, and around it centres much of the business. Into this harbour empties the Corrib, the outlet of the two great lakes, Lough Mask and Lough Corrib, a shallow, rocky, rushing

QUEEN'S COLLEGE, GALWAY.

stream, in which at certain seasons of the year the salmon are to be seen in such numbers that—to use the colloquial phrase—'you might walk across upon their backs.' The current is too rapid and the bed too shallow for navigation through the town, and the Eglinton Canal connects the harbour for traffic purposes with the upper part of the Corrib. Few rivers rival the Corrib in the abundance of salmon, and while every facility is afforded for legitimate sport, a good deal of poaching of the kind shown in the engraving on page 166 is there carried on, if report in this instance speaks truly.

At the mouth of the harbour, and forming the southernmost quarter of the town, is the Claddagh, a district inhabited solely by a clan of fishermen

and their families ; they live in low thatched huts, and are engaged for the
most part in the herring fishery. By some authorities they have been
considered of Spanish descent, while others, with more reason, hold that they
are of Celtic origin. ' The commerce between Galway and Spain was, no
doubt, at one time very extensive and important. The Spanish style of
many of the houses now in ruins, the traditions and authentic records, prove

SALMON POACHING ON THE CORRIB.
(From a sketch by Charles Whymper.)

that Galway was in old times a very thriving, busy, gay, and luxurious city.
No doubt many Spanish merchants lived in Galway, and intermarried with
natives long before the stern old Warden condemned his own son to death
for slaying a Spanish rival. A Spanish face may still be seen in and about
Galway once in a week or so ; but it appears to me quite certain that the
Claddagh, above all other people, had no intermarriage with Spaniards. In
proof of this, their present names are nearly all Irish, such as Connolly,

O'Connor, O'Flaherty; there are some English and Welsh, as Jones, Brown and Barrett; those first mentioned, however, form the great majority. The Christian names are generally Scriptural, as John, Matthew, Michael, Paul, also Patrick, Catharine, &c.; but they have this remarkable peculiarity, that there are so many persons of the same name that they are distinguished (in the Irish language) by the names of *fishes;* thus, Jack the *hake*, Bill the *cod*, Joe the *eel*, &c. The men and women of the Claddagh, and indeed of Galway County generally, are very fond of gay dress and bright colours; the country women often wear red cloaks, but the Claddagh women wear *blue* cloaks and *red* petticoats; the fishermen wear jacket, breeches and stockings home-made and *light blue*. The women often go bare foot, and wear the short blue cloak, bed-gown and red petticoat; the head dress is a kerchief of bright colours.

'There are no braver men at sea than the Claddagh fishermen, when they go off with the priestly benediction, and the blessed salt and ashes. On land, too, they can show courage when it is called forth and sustained by the consciousness of right. A few years ago they completely routed a considerable body of dragoons, by casting showers of heavy stones from their slings. By the way, casting pebbles from the sling is an amusement and a mode of warfare peculiar to the Claddagh men at the present day. Since the famine, this and other sports have been held in abeyance, but it was formerly usual for them to have "slinging matches"; and when a man was able to strike a shilling as far as it could be seen, it was considered a good shot. It must be refreshing to a Christian of any sect, who has seen much of the despairing infidelity and brutalizing wretchedness of some parts of England, to witness even the superstitions of this simple, patient, and joyous people. They believe in the actual presence of God among them, and do everything in His name. It is worthy of remark that they never by any chance salute or speak to each other without the name of God. I almost regretted to learn that the priests are discountenancing their old amiable superstitions. I may be excused for these allusions to the religion of this race, for certainly the thoughts and feelings of men form the most interesting phase of human study; and it might be a question with the social reformer whether these people in their ignorance and poverty are not happier than the rich, in whom the emotional element is comparatively dull, and who feel less acutely the joys and sorrows of the battle of life. Here in this remote west the historian also may see in fine preservation much of the life and feeling of the Middle Ages, while all is changed in the "go-ahead" world around. Like seamen everywhere, the Claddagh men have their lucky and unlucky

HOOK FOR POACHING SALMON.

days, and woe to him who dares to cast a line on an unpropitious morning. Formerly they would not on any account commence the fishing season unless the priest went along with them, and in regular form pronounced a blessing on the day, the boat with the priest sailing out at the head of the fleet.

'The appearance of the village of Claddagh is dirty, but the houses are clean enough inside ; and be it known that before the famine their houses were models of cleanliness ; and we must re-collect that those manure heaps which frequently offend the eye in Irish villages have no offensive odour, on account of the deodorizing power of the peat which forms a large portion of the compost. The men and women have gene-rally clean linen, although often covered with rags. It is a general fact worthy of note that in Ireland a dirty outside generally covers a clean heart.'[1]

Among the groups ga-thered at the fish market or clustering around Galway Harbour, the stranger will occasionally see men dressed like the one depicted in the engraving. He exhibits a facial type not common in the crowd, he wears very distinctive knee-breeches or knickerbockers, and his shoes, technically known as *pam-pootas*, are made of untanned cowhide with the hair left on, cut low at the

AN ARRAN ISLANDER.

(From a sketch by Charles Whymper.)

---

[1] *The Ulster Journal of Archæology*, vol. ii., pp. 162-165.

sides, with a narrow pointed piece to cover the toes.   It is said that
experience has proved that such shoes or sandals as these are best suited
for the rocky soil such men have to tread.   And when the stranger, his
curiosity aroused, desires to know whence these men come, he discovers
that they are from the Arran Islands.   These are three rocky islands
lying off the mouth of Galway Bay, abounding in ruins of the most
remarkable kind, and inhabited by a simple and kindly race of peasant
fishermen.   To describe in any detail the noted ruins upon these islands
would require a small volume.   The most famous is known as Dun Aengus.
It is a massive stone fort built in prehistoric times upon the very verge of
the western cliff of Inishmore, the largest of the group.   It is generally
conceded that this represents one of the last strongholds defended by the
original inhabitants of Ireland, and is supposed to date from about the first
century A.D.[1]   A steamer runs regularly to these islands, and they are full
of interest both to the antiquary, and to the tourist who ever yearns for
' fresh fields and pastures new.'

On these islands, at places like Barna, in Galway Bay, and in fact
almost universally along the western coast, the traveller meets and can readily
test the seaworthy qualities of the curragh, the representative of the ancient
coracle.   These boats, made of tarred canvas stretched over a light frame,
frail as they seem, can live in very rough weather, and are managed with
very great skill by the boatmen.   Their chief defect is that they make
much leeway when there is a strong breeze.   But any one who wishes to
make a voyage along this coast in much the same fashion as the Christian
missionaries in the fifth and sixth centuries, can do so by employing the
modern curragh.

After exhausting in a more or less rapid fashion the sights of Galway
and the neighbourhood, most travellers push on into the wilds of Connemara.
Loughs Corrib and Mask, together with the village of Cong, lie at the
beginning of the route.   During the summer a steamer sails daily from
Galway to Cong, traversing Lough Corrib, which is not only one of the
largest but also one of the loveliest in Ireland.   It covers an area of no
less than 44,000 acres.   It is studded with islets, the most important being
Inchagoill, or 'the island of the devout foreigner,' which contains an
ancient graveyard and the ruins of two very old Irish churches.   The
more ancient of the two is known as Teampull Phaidrig, or St. Patrick's
Church, and has claims by no means despicable to be considered as
belonging to the age of the great Irish missionary.   There is, moreover,
upon Inchagoill a stone monument bearing the inscription, ' the stone of
Lugnaedon, son of Limenueh,' who is generally held to have been sister of
St. Patrick.   Experts have decided that on palæographical grounds the

---

[1] Elaborate details with regard to the antiquarian relics on these islands are given in such works as Petrie's
Round Towers, Dunraven's *Notes on Irish Architecture*, and Miss Stokes' *Early Christian Architecture in Ireland*.

inscription cannot be referred to a later date than the very beginning of the sixth century.

The second church, Teampull-na-Neave, 'the church of the Saint,' is several centuries younger than St. Patrick's, and presents to the student of church architecture a very fine example of the decorated, circular-arched, cluster-pillared doorway.

On the isthmus connecting Loughs Corrib and Mask stands the village of Cong, the name being derived from the Irish word *Cunga*, which means 'a neck.' About the year 1010 Cong was the seat of a bishopric, and

THE CURRAGH.
(From sketches by Charles Whymper.)

there are still extant the ruins of a very fine abbey dating from the twelfth century. It belonged to the wealthy order of St. Augustine. During the last fifty or sixty years the remains have suffered severely from the depredations of those who considered and used it as a handy quarry. It was famous in early days for wealth and ecclesiastical treasures; of the latter the famous Cross of Cong, described on p. 44, is a good example. The Annals of the Four Masters record that in 'A.D. 1150 Muireadhach Ua Dubhthaigh, Archbishop of Connaught, chief senior of all Ireland in wisdom, chastity, in the bestowal of jewels and food, died at Cong in the 75th year of his age.' This man's name is inscribed upon the processional Cross of Cong.

Roderick O'Connor, who is often described as 'the last King of Ireland,' died here in 1198. The popular view, that he was also interred in Cong Abbey, is incorrect, he having been buried at Clonmacnois. But here he spent the last fifteen years of his life. 'Standing between the river and the abbey, the picture naturally rises before us of the ancient monarch, broken down by the calamities which his family was suffering from, a foreign invasion, which he was no longer able to resist, but still more so by the

CONG ABBEY.
(From a Photograph by Lawrence, of Dublin.)

opposition and ingratitude of his own children and relatives—passing up the river with his retinue, landing here in 1183, and received by the Lord Abbot and his canons and friars, and then taking leave of his faithful adherents at the water's edge, being conducted in procession to the abbey, which, it is said, his munificence had endowed. There as a recluse, untrammelled by the weight of state affairs, and possibly unaffected by the quarrels of his chieftains and kinsfolk, the Last Monarch of Ireland, abdicating his authority because the country no longer supported him, died,

THE OUTLET OF LOUGH MASK.

a sad but fitting and prophetic emblem of the
land over which he had ruled.'[1]

Not far from Cong is the Plain of Moytura,
where one of those famous battles—half-historic,
half-mythic—lasting three days, took place in the
dawn of Irish history between the Firbolgs and the Tuatha de Danaan.
Those who wish to get some accurate notion of what really took place on
that occasion cannot do better than consult Sir W. Wilde's *Lough Corrib*,
where they will find the history of the great struggle minutely traced.

[1] Sir W. Wilde's *Lough Corrib*, p. 181.

Lough Mask is about nine miles long and four wide, in a very beautiful part of the country, abounding in traces of ruined castles and churches. The river connecting the two lakes runs partly underground, and we are able to give an engraving of one part of this subterranean channel where it is easily accessible and widens out into what is known as the 'Pigeon Hole.' The lively Celtic imagination, which has produced all over Ireland such a rich crop of fairy lore and local legends, has enriched the stream with a brace of holy white trout, which it would be impious in the extreme to catch.

And now, turning our course westwards, one of the most picturesque

GLENDALOUGH.

regions of Connaught lies before us. It is the fashion to rush this district by aid of tourist cars. It is hardly needful to say that a more leisurely progress, even if it lead to the expense of private cars, will soon repay the traveller for the expenditure of time and money. The first half of the 47 miles that separate Clifden from Galway are not particularly interesting; but when Oughterard and Lough Shindilla is reached, the excursion becomes one to delight the lover of fine scenery. To the north rise the Mamturk Mountains, 2,000 feet high; then comes the valley known as Glen Inagh, at the entrance to which stands the huge sentinel,

Lissoughter, 1,314 feet high. From the summit of this hill a superb view is obtained over Glen Inagh, Lough Inagh and the wild mountain road to the north-west leading to Kylemore. The chief feature in the view, however, is the cluster of mountain peaks to the north-west, the celebrated Pins of Bunnabeola.

Under the shadow of Lissoughter the road skirts the shores of

THE PINS OF BUNNABEOLA.

Glendalough, a lovely lake, but, like Killarney, apt to suffer somewhat from the extreme claims put forth on its behalf by too enthusiastic admirers. From this point onwards the road to Clifden runs through a succession of valleys either by the side of a rippling mountain stream or along the delightful shores of Glendalough and Derryclare and Ballynahinch. Dominating the whole western half of the drive, and affording a succession of delightful mountain views, stands the cluster of 'peaks of Beola,' the word 'bin' or 'ben,' 'mountain,' having been corrupted into 'pin.' Benbaun, the highest of the group, is 2,395 feet above the sea level.

Clifden is a well-situated little town, standing at the head of Ardbear Bay, and shut in to the north and east by a circle of mountains. There is not much trade carried on here, and this whole district has never recovered fully from the terrible famine experiences. But on a market day the crowd of peasants and the various business transactions present much that catches the attention of a stranger. The women in blue or scarlet cloaks, the men in frieze coats and knee-breeches, the pigs and sheep, the lively actions and conversations, all combine to make up a picturesque and animated

KYLEMORE.

scene. The best excursion from Clifden is through the Martin country to Roundstone and Urrisberg, a hill which although only 987 feet high, yet from its isolated position affords a lovely view, and presents phenomena interesting alike to the botanist and geologist.

Those who follow the beaten track, after staying the night at Clifden, will proceed by car another 40 miles to Westport. This route also carries the traveller through some magnificent scenery. Soon after reaching Letterfrack, the Pass of Kylemore is entered. If a choice had to be made among the many exquisite scenes of this region, not a few would award the palm to Kylemore. From Letterfrack the Pass of Salrock and Lough Fee are easily reached, and lovely views obtained over the Killary, an arm of the sea running inland for 12 miles, and often compared to a Norwegian fjord. An even better centre is Leenane, beautifully situated at the head of Killary Harbour. From thence a whole series of most delightful excursions can be made. By ascending Mwcelrea, on the north shore of Killary Harbour, 2,688 feet high, a superb view is obtained. A charming and less fatiguing trip is to Delphi and Lough Doo. The valley of the Errif, Lough Natooey, and many other parts of this pleasant region, afford the best of sport to the angler. Lough Natooey is famed for its gillaroo trout. The main road to Westport continues up the Errif Valley and across the watershed into the valley of the Owenwee. During the ride some grand views are obtained over Clew Bay.

Westport, like other towns on this coast, is prepared on a somewhat ambitious scale for a prosperous future, which has not yet arrived. It is situated at the head of Westport Bay, an inlet of Clew Bay. It is certainly beautiful for situation, and hard by is the lovely park of the Marquis of Sligo. Beyond this is Westport Quay, with its warehouses and wharfs, but having nothing wherewith to fill them. To the south and west the prominent feature in every view is Croagh Patrick, the lofty conical mountain whence, according to tradition, St. Patrick finally cleared Ireland of reptiles. The mountain has long been the scene of pilgrimages. But in these days it is quite sufficient to rest its claims to attention upon purely natural features. The view from the summit, about 2,500 feet high, embraces a glorious prospect over Achill Island to the Donegal Highlands, over the whole expanse of Clew Bay with its thousand islets, and over the mountain regions of Connemara.

A visit to Clare Island enables the visitor to appreciate the fine scenery of the bay, and also to see the ruins of the castle where the famous Amazon Grace O'Malley is said to have resided in Queen Elizabeth's day.

The road from Westport to Newport affords fine views of Clew Bay along the eight miles separating the two places. Here another excursion, much more elaborate and needing more time, for which Newport is a good starting-point, is the trip to Achill Island. To do this with any comfort, three or four days are necessary. The rapid tourist might do much in two days or two and a half. Achill is the largest island off the Irish coast, having a shore-line of some 80 miles, and containing 46,000 acres. A long drive from Newport leads to the ferry at Achill Sound, and a further run of nine miles to Dugort, the best centre for exploration. Hence excursions may be planned according to the time and strength of the traveller. Slievemore, 2,217 feet high, overhangs Dugort. At the hamlets of Keel, Dooagh and Keem, a good idea can be obtained of aboriginal life. The people live in round cabins, looking at a distance like corn ricks; they use the curragh, and are simple and primitive in habit. Here may be seen to perfection fishing for salmon with a seine. The salmon on their way to the rivers travel round the bays. A man perched on the crags, who, by reason of the clearness of the water and the whiteness of the bottom, can see every movement of the fish, directs the men when and where to haul the seine so as to enclose the greatest number of fish. This method is followed in other parts of Connaught, and we are able to give an illustrative engraving of the process.

The two special things for which many visit Achill are to see the seal caves and to look down Croghan. The caves are visited by boat, and are about two miles from Dugort. If the trip is made when the animals

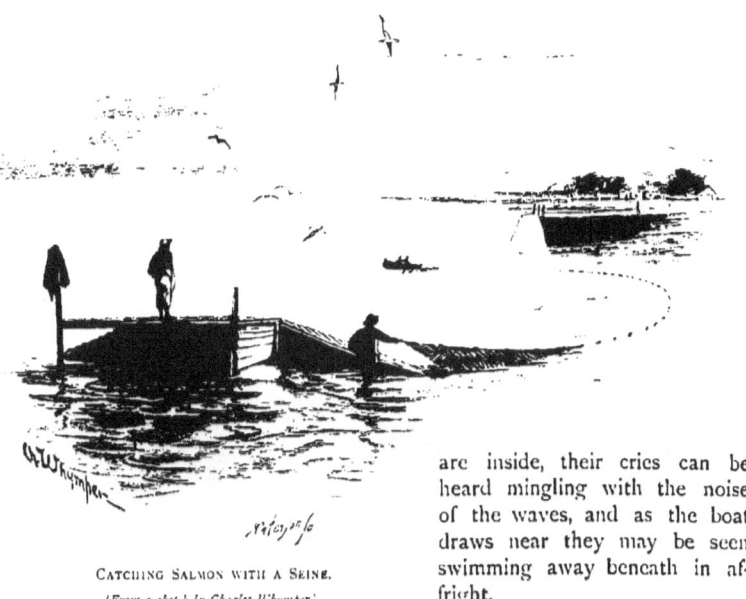

CATCHING SALMON WITH A SEINE.

(From a sketch by Charles Whymper.)

are inside, their cries can be heard mingling with the noise of the waves, and as the boat draws near they may be seen swimming away beneath in affright.

The Croghan is a long range of cliff forming the west coast of Achill. The approach from the land side is gradual, but when the proper point is reached by creeping cautiously to the edge and looking over, the explorer can gaze down 2,000 feet of sheer precipice. 'The mountain seemed to have been rent in twain by some stupendous convulsion of Nature, and half its mass to have dropped bodily into the ocean. We stood on the summit, and below us the Atlantic surged and roared, beating on the jagged rocks, and sending columns of white foam high into the air. It made us giddy to look down the face of the cliffs.

N

In some places the rocks under us were hidden from our view, as they
toppled over the sea at an angle of sixty degrees.   In the recesses of

KILLALA.

these mighty cliffs, which extend their bare crags against the sea for five
miles, from Saddle Head to Achill Head, numbers of golden eagles have

their eyries, and flocks of wild goats have their habitation, affording sport that equals chamois hunting in its danger and excitement, and requires the sure foot of the mountaineer and the skill of the deerstalker.' '

From Achill Island the traveller may return to Newport and journey north through a fine district, past Mount Nephin and Lough Conn to Ballina. Or—and by this route he will see the less known parts of County Mayo— he can skirt Blacksod Bay, and reach Ballina by way of Belmullet, Ballycastle, and Killala.

The last-named is an interesting little place, the seat of a bishopric which is now united with that of Tuam, and famed for the fact that the French landed here in 1798. The see is very ancient, dating from the fifth century. The present cathedral is a seventeenth century building, occupying the site of the old sixth century church. The Round Tower is a very ancient structure. Formerly Killala was a busy port, but in recent years most of the trade has gone to Ballina. Between these two places are the ruins of Moyne Abbey.

At Ballina the railway is reached, and the traveller feels himself once more in touch with the facilities of advanced civilization, and can extend his wanderings into Donegal, or reluctantly, if he must, turn his face homewards.

¹ *Midland Great Western Railway Handbook*, p. 51.

GOING TO MARKET.

DONEGAL CASTLE.

CHAPTER VIII.

THE DONEGAL HIGHLANDS.

THE Donegal Highlands offer many and great attractions to the stranger. He finds there much wild and enticing mountain scenery; he can explore a magnificent coast, indented by numerous loughs and arms of the sea, and adorned by a succession of bold headlands; he treads a land classic in Irish story, and renowned for the men who there took part in both internecine struggles and in the conflict with the Saxon race; and he finds in the people of to-day a primitive and most interesting peasantry. He can visit the scenes of Columba's boyhood, and of Hugh Roe's brave efforts for freedom. If interested in political and social questions, he can study typical

CARRIGAN HEAD, DONEGAL.

representatives of landlord and tenant, and typical conflicts between the National League and Dublin Castle. He will find the Celtic imagination even more lively in Donegal than in most parts with a firm belief in fairies, and in a store of legends associated with mountain and river, castle and hamlet.

Great are the charms of Wicklow and Kerry, manifold are the beauties of Mayo and Antrim; yet upon any one who wishes to see Ireland at its best, that is, as least affected by outside influences, Donegal should have the prior claim. More than equal to her rivals in natural beauty, there is also a stronger element of the 'mere Irish' in the people, and in their habits of life.

THE EAST WINDOW, SLIGO ABBEY.

THE CLOISTERS, SLIGO ABBEY.

Continuing our journey from Ballina, the best approach is by way of Sligo and Ballyshannon. The former is an important county town, well-situated and fairly prosperous. Lough Gill, a lovely sheet of water, dotted with islands, is only a few miles distant, the waters of its only outlet flowing through the town. There is a considerable shipping trade, since Sligo is a port, and stands at the head of a fine bay. Like almost every Irish town of importance, it contains an ancient ruined monastery. This was founded by the Earl of Kildare in the thirteenth century, but the fine ruins which all visitors to Sligo should inspect are those of the monastery and church, rebuilt after a fire early in the fifteenth century. These are of considerable extent, the choir of the church exhibiting a splendid four-light east window, and the unusually perfect cloisters being worthy of careful study, since they have many richly decorated arches which enable the student to appreciate the native Irish school of architecture.

Passing through Bundoran, Ballyshannon is reached, noted for its salmon fishery and its falls. These are 150 yards wide and from fourteen to sixteen feet high, and over them the waters of Lough Erne find an outlet. The chief sight at Ballyshannon in the proper season is the salmon making their way up these falls. Only a few miles from the town is Belleck, the site of the celebrated pottery works, where a very beautiful and delicate china ware, possessing a rich iridescent lustre, has for many years been manufactured. The works are not so prosperous as formerly, but all who know the excellence of the pottery trust that the depression will prove to be but temporary. Lough Erne and Lough Derg are both within easy reach of Ballyshannon, the latter having been for ages a famous place of pilgrimage. By road Donegal is only a little over thirty miles from Sligo, but in order to reach it by rail a circuit covering a considerable part of Ireland is needful. The journey ranks high among picturesque railway trips. The train traverses the rich district of Manor Hamilton, and enables the traveller to visit one of the most noted and best-situated towns—Enniskillen. Lough Erne is an expansion of the River Erne, forming a lovely and most extensive lake, which takes very high rank for natural beauty. About midway it contracts into a narrow stream, and upon this Enniskillen stands, eminently beautiful for situation. Two miles below the town is Devenish Island, with a Round Tower and old ruined abbey. On leaving Enniskillen the railway continues through Omagh and Newtown Stewart to Strabane, and there the branch to Donegal turns off abruptly to the west and southwest, passing through the Barnesmore Gap, a fine gorge through the mountains, which rise on one side over 1,700 feet, and on the other over 1,400 feet. The rail extends only to Druminin, two or three miles from Donegal, the journey thither being completed by car, the ride giving a good foretaste of the pleasures to come in the way of beautiful views.

The town, which has given its name to the county, stands at the head of the great arm of the sea called Donegal Bay. The word is Irish, and means *Dun-nan-Gal*, 'the fort of the stranger,' and the name is comparatively modern. In ancient days all this region was known as Tyrconnell, that is, the Land of Connel or Conall, a son or Nial of the Nine Hostages. The houses for the most part cluster around a central space called the Diamond ; but although Donegal is a port and a county town, there are not many signs of business activity. There are only two structures of special note, the castle and the monastery, both in ruins. Each is associated in a most interesting way with the history of the country. To fairly appreciate the

castle, a glance must be taken at ancient history. A little before the time
when St. Patrick worked as a slave in Antrim there ruled over Ireland one
of the most celebrated of pagan kings, Niall of the Nine Hostages. Two
of his sons, Conall and Eoghan (Owen) settled in the north, and gave their
names to the districts of Tyr-conall and Tyr-coghan (Tyrone), and became
respectively the ancestors of the powerful Ulster Septs, the O'Donnells and
O'Neils. From the thirteenth to the fifteenth centuries internecine war
raged fiercely between these great clans, a fact which here, as in other parts
of the kingdom, facilitated its subjugation by England. About the middle
of the fifteenth century Hugh Roe became chief of the O'Donnells, and in
1474 founded the Franciscan monastery at Donegal. In the latter part of
the sixteenth century it had become customary for each chieftain in turn to
seek English support, for the purpose of attacking the other. In 1585 Sir
John Perrott, the Lord Deputy, divided Ulster into counties, decreeing that
Tyrconnell should in future be known as Donegal. Hugh O'Donnell, the
head of the Sept at that time, vehemently resisted this policy. He was an
old man, and becoming feeble. His son Hugh, who was a prince of great
promise, happened to be staying, according to the Irish custom, with his
foster-father, MacSweeny, at Fanad. Thinking that they could manage
the old O'Donnell more easily than the young one, the English determined
to get the latter out of the way. He was enticed on board a ship at
Rathmullan on Lough Swilly, made prisoner and carried to Dublin Castle.
In 1590, after more than three years' imprisonment, he escaped, but was
recaptured. In 1592 he and a prince of the rival Sept of O'Neils escaped,
but lost their way during a snowstorm in Glenmalure, County Wicklow ; the
O'Neil died, Hugh Roe was rescued, and brought back from the point of
death, and finally reached Donegal in safety. His feelings towards the
English can easily be imagined. He became head of the Sept on the
resignation of his father, made his home at Donegal Castle, and at once
attacked the English in Tyrone. In 1597 he captured Ballyshannon ; in
1598 he aided Hugh O'Neil to defeat the English at the Yellow Ford, two
miles from Armagh ; in 1599 he defeated the English at Ballaghboy, and
slew their leader, Sir Conyers Clifford. But treachery was too strong in the
end even for Hugh Roe. He was deserted, at the time when he most
needed support, by his brother-in-law, Nial Garv, who joined the English in
attacking him. After performing brilliant deeds in the ensuing struggle, he
went at length to Spain, to seek help from Philip III. Help was freely
promised, but never came. Hugh Roe waited, and waited in vain, at
Corunna for the fleet, strong enough to liberate Ulster, that was to bear him
back to Ireland. His fiery spirit wore out its casket. Starting for the
court to urge once more his suit before the King, at Simancas he was seized
with fatal illness, died in the King's house there, and was honoured with a
splendid burial in the cathedral of Valladolid, on September 10th 1602. At

the time of his death he was only twenty-eight years old. Thus closed a most romantic, brilliant and courageous career. Among the multitude of fierce, agile, and warlike chieftains of Ireland Hugh Roe holds one of the highest places.

It is with the fortunes of this chief and his immediate ancestors that the old Donegal Castle was concerned. The original structure was built by the Hugh O'Donnell who was ruling Tyrconnell in 1505, but little or nothing of this building survives. The extant ruins are those of the castle rebuilt upon the old foundation by Sir Basil Brooke in 1610. When complete it must have been a fine specimen of its class, consisting chiefly of a tall, gabled tower, with turrets and the necessary out-buildings. The greater part of the tower is still standing. The chief room in it possesses a very fine mullioned window and a splendid chimney-piece. The situation is charming, the castle being surrounded by a lovely garden, and overhanging the river Esk.

The monastery, of which only the scantiest remains exist, was founded in 1474. When Nial Garv betrayed the cause of Hugh Roe he seized and fortified this monastery. There he was attacked by his brother-in-law, and a fire happening to break out, Hugh Roe seized upon that moment as the time for an assault, in which Nial was defeated and driven out, and the monastery reduced to ruin. Some years later the friars began to gather again upon the old spot, and built themselves some cottages amongst the ruins. In these cottages was compiled the most famous of those great Annals for which Irish literature is so noted, viz., the *Annals of the Four Masters*. The book was so called because it was the work of four friars of great learning, the chief being Michael O'Leary, a native of Ballyshannon. The work these four men produced consists of 11,000 quarto pages, begins with the year of the world, 2242, and closes with A.D. 1616. The Annals are made up largely of brief details and records of battles, of the foundation and destruction of churches and abbeys, and of the deaths of chieftains, kings, abbots, &c.; nevertheless they form a priceless storehouse of information about Irish history. In recent years these Annals have been twice edited, the last edition being a handsomely printed book in four large quarto volumes.

Donegal is the gate to the beautiful southern district of the county. The ride along the north coast of Donegal Bay is exceedingly lovely. Fine sea views are obtained on the one hand, and on the other very extensive and very fine mountainous landscapes everywhere occur. The mail-car route to Killybegs is a splendid example of a fine Irish road. The first place of interest is Mount Charles, situated on the slope of a hill, from which, above the village, a most magnificent view is obtained over the demesne of the Marquis of Conyngham, over the bay, and over the wild highland region of the Blue Stack Mountains, and on very favourable days

even the Connaught coast may be clearly seen in the distant south. Passing
by Bruckless, a pretty village, and leaving the ruins of MacSwyne's Castle
on the left hand, after a pleasant ride of some miles, Killybegs is reached.
This is a snug little seaport, well situated on the shore of a fine land-locked
harbour. The road from this place to Kilcar hugs the coast at a considerable elevation above the sea, and thus affords the traveller a constant
succession of superb views. He is, of course, largely dependent upon the
weather. If the sun be shining, nothing can be more delightful than this
ride; and even if it be seen through a Donegal 'smirr' (a drizzling rain)—
and here the writer speaks from experience—it can still impart pleasure to

DONEGAL.

(From a photograph by Lawrence, of Dublin.)

the traveller. Not far from Kilcar
is Muckross, a mountain nearly 1,000
feet high, with a promontory jutting
out boldly into the sea. The rocks
here, and especially the mass known as the Market House, will delight the
lover of cliff scenery. Yet all but leisurely travellers will be eager to push
on to Slieve League, now only a few miles distant. The road after leaving
Kilcar crosses the Ballyduff River, passes over a high moorland—and if the
traveller meets the 'smirr' here he is apt to remember it—and then runs
along the eastern bank of Teelin Bay and River, with splendid views of
the bay in the foreground, and with the mighty mass of Slieve League
shutting in the distant view across the valley. At the village of Carrick
most comfortable hotel accommodation is to be found, and no better centre
for the exploration of the Slieve League district could be desired.

188   *IRISH PICTURES.*

For this country, fine weather is almost essential; but, alas! it is not often granted to those whose time is limited. In short, it cannot be too strongly emphasized that, in order to enjoy Donegal scenery properly, time is essential. A fair idea may be obtained by rushing through the county, and if the visitor has to choose between seeing it under these conditions and not seeing it at all, the author would say by all means visit it even thus. But let all who wish really to enjoy what is unquestionably the freshest, most unconventional, and in many respects most beautiful part of the Emerald Isle, allot considerable time to it. Three weeks or a month spent in doing Donegal thoroughly will be at once a better education in appreciating Ireland and the Irish, and a more complete rest to the mind than six weeks spent in skimming over the greater part of the kingdom. The full enjoyment of a visit to Slieve League, for instance—and by this is meant the careful and repeated study of these stupendous cliffs, with all their rich colouring, and the grand views afforded from different points of vantage, and the leisurely exploration of the five or six miles of headlands, in order to appreciate the wondrous variety of expression they present—can only be obtained in fine weather, and by an expenditure of at least two or three days. The changes of weather, also, are very rapid. A seemingly hopeless day will often rapidly clear, and the visitor, not too much hampered by dates and the daily tale of completed miles, can avail himself of these changes.

Slieve League is a huge mountain mass, presenting on the land side lofty slopes and valleys, but no forms that specially strike the eye. The sea face has been beaten by the storms of ages into the most superb cliffs in the British Islands. The easiest and best method of exploring it is to walk or drive along the west bank of the Teelin River for a couple of miles, and then turn up the path leading to what is known as Bunglas. The path winds up by easy ascents through a valley leading at length to Carrigan Head. This is a magnificent piece of cliff scenery, a suitable introduction to the greater wonders beyond.

Leaving Carrigan Head on the left, and following the path which winds along the cliffs, Bunglas is soon reached, and one instantly appreciates why the spot obtained the name Awark-Mor, meaning 'the fine view.' The visitor stands upon a point of rock, many hundreds of feet above the sea level. From his right hand there sweeps away a grand semicircle of cliff, rising higher and higher above the sea until opposite where the observer stands it reaches an altitude of nearly 2,000 feet. Beyond this point, the cliffs stretch away for six miles, extending to Malin Beg and Malin More. The sharp bend in the cliffs to the observer's right is sometimes called 'the lair of the whirlwinds,' and the face of the cliffs is exceedingly fine. Their very extent detracts to a large degree from the impressiveness of their height, and it is hard at first to realise that the wave breaking slowly at the foot is, in some places, almost perpendicularly 2,000 feet below the crown of the ridge. Unlike the lofty cliffs of Kerry, this gigantic wall is warm in its colouring. Reddish tints abound, and quartz veins, and bands of shining white quartz, bared and polished by the storms of untold ages, combined with the red-brown bogs, and green mosses, produce colours, which contrast magnificently with the water below and the sky above. Undoubtedly the best way to comprehend the full grandeur of the cliffs is to come round by boat from Teelin Point; but for this trip the finest weather is essential.

The summit of Slieve League is reached by a narrow way known as 'One Man's Path.' About this the most conflicting reports had reached the author. Some described it as a path needing the steadiest nerve, while a gentleman thoroughly familiar with every peak in Donegal, a practised mountain climber, described it as a place one could run down. Great, therefore, was his disappointment when, having reached Bunglas, and fully hoping to test the accuracy of these conflicting accounts, a dense cloud which had persistently rested upon the summit, hiding completely from view the last 200 or 300 feet of the ascent, not only grew denser, but transformed itself into a persistent driving rain. Under these circumstances, he had to leave unsolved the question whether he could easily walk up the 'One Man's Path,' or whether it was an expedition needing a combination of careful guide and steady nerve. It was a melancholy satisfaction to note, some hours later, when he caught his last glimpse of Slieve League from the Kilcar Road, that the heavy cloud still shrouded the top of the mountain, and there was every evidence that the rain was descending even more heavily than when he stood at Bunglas.

The view from Bunglas, once seen, must ever remain a glorious memory. It is also much finer, because more picturesque, than that obtained from the summit, since there the greater part of the mighty cliff wall is hidden. The top is reached by 'a path from Bunglas along the verge of the precipice the whole way up to the top of the mountain. On approaching the summit line, the visitor will find that the mountain narrows to an edge, called the One Man's Path, from the circumstance that they who are bold enough to tread it must pass in single file over the sharp ridge. On the land side, an escarpment, not indeed vertical, but steep enough to seem so from above, descends more than 1,000 feet to the brink of a small tarn; while on the side facing the sea the precipices descend from 1,300 to 1,800 feet, literally straight as a wall, to the ocean. A narrow footway, high in the air, with both these awful abysses yawning on either side, is the One Man's Path, which in the language and imagination of the people of the district is the special characteristic of Slieve League, a distinction that it surely merits. . . . The view is worthy of this great maritime Alp. Southwards you take in a noble horizon of mountains ranging from Leitrim to the Stags of Broadhaven, and in the dim distance are seen Nephin above Ballina, and, when the atmosphere is peculiarly clear, Croagh Patrick, above Westport. Looking inland you behold a sea of mountain-tops receding in tumultuous waves as far as the rounded head of Slieve Snaght, and the sharp cone of Errigal. . . . A quarry lately opened shows this part of the mountain to be formed of piles of thin small flags of a beautiful white colour, thus proving, what the geologist would have seen at the first glance, that those quadrilateral pillars standing straight up from the steeply escarped side, and called *chimneys* by the people, are portions of the formation of the precipice which have not yet wholly yielded to the atmospheric action that has worn the rest into a slope. And here observe how much there is in a name; for Slieve League (or Liaga) means the Mountain of Flags.'[1]

Continuing this, probably the finest coast walk in the United Kingdom, past Malin Beg, and Malin More, Glen Bay is reached, which ultimately becomes Glencolumbcille. That St. Columba was born at Gartan in Donegal, in A.D. 521, seems beyond doubt; that he once lived in this glen has been accepted by many as a fact, although Dr. Reeves, in his splendid edition of Adamnan's *Life of the Saint*, treats it as a late legend. Some even maintain that the time-worn cross in the churchyard was originally placed there by the founder of Iona. However these things may be, the Glen is a part of the country that no one should miss.

From this point two roads are open to Ardara. The most frequented, that through Carrick, we shall touch upon later. The wilder and much less common is to follow the coast, passing by the Sturrel, commonly known as the Bent Cliff, an extraordinary mass of rock jutting out from the precipices which here form the coast line, and rounding the slopes of Slieveatooey, with Loughros Beg Bay and Loughros More Bay immediately beneath.

This is a fitting place to refer to the Donegal peasantry. We are able to give an engraving of a group. They are a fine sturdy race, well-made and seemingly well-fed. There are not the evident signs of mental quickness so readily seen in some districts of Ireland, and the hints that life is a hard struggle with poverty are abundant. But they are self-reliant and free from all tendency to cringe. They are not forward to make advances, but they respond readily to the kindly look or the civil word. Until recently, perhaps more than in many parts, they were strongly swayed by their landlords, and on this account possibly the Home Rule feeling runs very strongly among them. But they do not obtrude this side of their life upon the passing stranger. The author's experience of them exactly coincides with that of the writer of *An Unknown Country:* 'We saw in returning family groups sitting by the roadside on the moor or chatting outside their cabin doors. They just glanced up as we drove past, nothing more. There was nothing of the wild pursuit of tourists by child-

[1] *The Donegal Highlands,* pp. 99 100.

beggars—and grown-up beggars too—and nothing of the fierce scowl at all supposed well-to-do people, which I had been told we should find in this land ripe for revolution. And though they were as poor as poor could be —a poverty which our English poor could hardly realize—they all looked *respectable;* a word which implies more than at first appears, since a man who is worthy of respect must first respect himself. They would have been a problem to many English who pass rash and harsh judgments upon Ireland. . . . Nothing strikes one more in Donegal, or indeed, throughout Ireland,

DONEGAL PEASANTS.
(From a photograph by Lawrence, of Dublin.)

than the exceeding wholesomeness of the children. Ragged they may be, thin, and half-starved, but they are seldom either crippled or diseased. They can run like hares, and spring like wild-cats; they look up at you fearlessly with their big, bright, Irish eyes, and grin at you with their dazzling teeth, till you laugh in spite of yourself, and they laugh back again, as if, in spite of all this misery, life were a capital joke."

If the coast route is not followed in the journey from Carrick to Ardara, and the beaten track is chosen, a very fine stretch of bleak moorland country is traversed. The road gradually rises, the country getting wilder and wilder, until at an elevation of about 1,000 feet the highest point is reached, and immediately below is the Pass of Glengesh, while spread out before one is a fine view of the central Donegal Mountains. The crest once surmounted, the road descends rapidly by abrupt turns into the glen, the hills towering aloft on either hand. The scenery gets less and less wild as the road descends, and the valley towards the mouth becomes smiling and green and fertile. A short run brings the car into Ardara, and ascending the steep hillside on which the main street of this little town stands the road to Glenties is reached. An hour's ride along the slope of a pleasant valley brings one to the town, which owes its importance mainly to the fact that it is a convenient place for changing horses. A handsome workhouse is the great architectural feature of the place; several mountain glens and the roads passing through them converge upon it; but there is little connected with it to tempt the wayfarer into any lengthy stay.

Between Glenties and Gweedore a long stretch of extremely wild and barren country intervenes, so wild and bare as to be hardly rivalled in the United Kingdom. The absence of wood and foliage intensifies the impression of barrenness. What picturesque effect it possesses is due mainly to the hill contours, and to the shades of moorland browns, varied with occasional oases of living green, often entirely due to large patches of *Osmunda regalis*, the royal, flowering fern. Seen, as not unfrequently, beneath a grey sky and with a keen east wind blowing, the visitor on the jaunting car is apt to think that Irish miles in these parts are abnormally long, and that in the course of his wanderings over the face of the earth he has never traversed a more hopeless soil or a more thinly populated country.

The first point of real beauty in the journey is when the road touches the valley of the Gweebarra, a fine salmon stream, emptying into Gweebarra Bay. The road for some miles skirts the southern bank, which is bleak and barren; but on the opposite side the valley rolls away in gentle slopes, dotted plentifully with whitewashed cabins, and cultivated fields, supporting evidently a considerable agricultural population. At Doochary Bridge the road crosses the river, and immediately climbs by zig-zags the steep northern bank. From the top some very fine views are obtained; and then for seven or eight miles the road traverses wild moors.

Dungloe is a village nestling on the slope of a hill, but neither beautiful for situation nor particularly attractive in itself. The road to Gweedore, some thirteen miles, is very pleasant, and affords considerable variety of scenery, but is not comparable to several that Donegal can show. By far the finest drive from Glenties to Gweedore is to go by way of Doochary Bridge and Glen Veagh, a longer but a much wilder route. But the best way to appreciate the Errigal district is to make the Gweedore Hotel a centre and explore the country by daily excursions.

Gweedore is situated upon the Clady, a pretty stream forming the outlet of a chain of loughs. The most conspicuous object in the landscape is Mount Errigal, only a few miles distant, and very accessible. It presents widely different appearances from different points of view; from Gweedore itself looking like a dome; from other directions exhibiting the sharp ridge and bold peak shown in our engraving. Scattered over the slopes are immense quantities of a loose shale of a pure white colour, which, seen from a distance, have almost the effect of snow. On the south-eastern side the peak slopes down by a sharp ridge, which affords a capital path up to the very summit. The height is 2,460 feet, and any fair walker can easily manage the ascent. The writer first saw it on a bright sunny afternoon in June, towards the close of a long drive from Creeslough. It looked so

MOUNT ERRIGAL.
(*From a photograph by Lawrence, of Dublin.*)

inviting and so easy to climb that the temptation was irresistible. Instructing the car-driver to wait, he started, and at once met the chief difficulties of the expedition. The ground at the foot of the mountain is boggy, and some care is needed in crossing the half mile or so of nearly level ground. But once on the ridge the rest was easy. The view from the summit was superb. The complete isolation of the peak, the extreme abruptness with which the mountain slopes away in all directions but one, and the grandeur of the surrounding peaks, render the enjoyment of being actually on the summit exceedingly keen and invigorating. The eye is bewildered at first by the vast extent and variety of the landscape unfolded. Looking to the north and east, the mountain seems to break away almost from beneath one's feet, and although it is at least a mile from the base,

Altan Lough looks so near that you think the stone in your hand could be easily tossed into it. Beyond the lough the steep cliffs of Aghla More rise up abruptly for nearly 2,000 feet, and beyond them towers the huge mass of Muckish, the mountain that dominates all North-western Donegal. Far away in the distance, Mulroy Bay, Lough Swilly, and the blue ocean are in full view. Immediately to the north and east, Dunfanaghy, Horn Head and Tory Island seem to lie at one's feet. To the south the fine ranges of the Derryveagh Mountains, the Poisoned Glen, and Slieve Snaght, separated from the observer only by the narrow valley in which are nestled Loughs Dunlewy and Nacung, stretch out to the right and left, while beyond them is an ever-widening circle of mountains, bounded on the west by the restless Atlantic, and stretching away to the south and east as far as the eye can reach. No finer view exists in Ireland than the wondrous panorama stretched out before the observer who sits upon the topmost peak of Errigal, and no better position for rapidly acquiring the topography of Donegal could possibly be desired. Although the side of the mountain facing Dunlewy looks dangerously steep when viewed from below, the writer had no difficulty in descending on that side, and rejoined his car after an absence of two hours.

No visitor to Gweedore should miss Glenveagh, the most famous of Donegal valleys. The way to see it in all respects to the best advantage is to take a car from Gweedore, drive past Lough Nacung, and the southern side of Errigal, through what is known as the valley of the Calabber. From the water-shed separating the valleys of the Owenbeg and the Calabber a grand mountain view is obtained. On the left Errigal, Aghla More, Aghla Beg, and Muckish lift up their mighty masses ; on the right stand the peak and slopes of Mount Dooish, and in front a fine distant view is obtained over Creeslough. Some miles beyond this crest the road turns to the right, crosses the Glenveagh river and runs for some miles along the southern shore of Lough Veagh. Near the further end of the lough stands a modern building, a blot rather than an adornment to the landscape, known as the Castle. Beyond the Castle the road winds along at the foot of a well-wooded slope. The opposite bank of both lough and glen are much wilder. The mountains descend for a thousand feet nearly sheer to the water, or to the level of the valley. At one part a beautiful cascade runs like a snow-white thread down the face of the cliff. Ascending still further the scene grows wilder and wilder. Here the car should be left to return to Dunlewy, and the rest of the trip made on foot. A magnificent walk enables the pedestrian to hit the head of the Poisoned Glen, a wild and rugged valley directly opposite to Mount Errigal, and to descend through it rejoining the Gweedore Road at Dunlewy. By this route a constant succession of most beautiful mountain views is enjoyed.

Dunfanaghy, some seventeen miles from Gweedore, is an interesting

O 2

THE NATURAL ARCH, HORN HEAD.

From a Photograph by Lawrence, of Dublin.

little town with a capital hotel, and a considerable amount of life about it, by reason of the mail and tourist traffic with Letterkenny. The two lions of the district are Horn Head and Tory Island. The former is a huge promontory jutting out into the Atlantic, equipped with all the needful qualities to charm the eye and satisfy adventurous spirits bent upon exploration, viz., bold cliffs rising from 500 to 700 feet above the sea, caves which can only be visited by boat, natural arches and a great puffing hole known as MacSwyne's Gun. Horn Head, so called because when seen from a certain point of view the cliff seems to possess two horns, forms a kind of *ultima thule*, and ranks high among the famous points of the Donegal coast. We give an engraving of a splendid natural arch to be seen on the western cliffs of Horn Head. MacSwyne's Gun is a rocky cavern open at the top, through which the sea at times forces waves with such tremendous violence that great blocks of stone are hurled up on the shore with a noise which, according to the natives, can be heard thirty miles!

Tory Island is about eight miles distant from the coast, and is inhabited by a race of fishermen possessed of striking peculiarities, like the Arran Islanders. It also contains a ruined Round Tower, and a monastery is said to have been founded on the island by Columba. It is not an easy place to reach, as the author found, for although an expedition had been kindly planned for him, the weather did not prove propitious. We could have reached the island, but the boatmen were by no means certain when we should be able to return. In fact, the best view I had of it was when from the peak of Errigal it looked like a lovely gem set in the brilliant blue of the Atlantic, and appeared to be only two or three instead of fifteen or twenty miles away. It is about three miles long and one wide, containing about 1,200 acres, of which 200 can be cultivated. At the north-western end there is a fine lighthouse. The inhabitants live by fishing, by agriculture, and by kelp-making; the last occupation is common to many parts of the Irish coast, and consists of collecting sea-weed on the beach and burning it into kelp, which was formerly purchased because of its iodine-producing qualities. The inhabitants naturally are skilful in the management of the curragh.

From Dunfanaghy there are two routes open to the traveller. The least interesting is by the mail road to Letterkenny, where he touches civilization again in the form of the railroad. The other is to make his way around the great inlets of the Atlantic on the north coast of Donegal until he reaches Lough Swilly. This route, unless he happens to be familiar with the country and people, or to have the assistance of local friends, is somewhat rough, and is only to be recommended to those who rate making the acquaintance of new country and truly primitive people a higher pleasure than the mere enjoyment of creature comforts. Such will find the district of Fanet between Dunfanaghy and Port Salon on Lough Swilly a happy hunting-ground. Sheephaven is the first of these great

arms of the sea which have to be skirted, the road passing Creeslough, then
running along by the Duntally River and crossing the Lackagh, that river
famous not only for its salmon, but for a great law-suit in the time of the
late Lord Leitrim. Ards House, the mansion belonging to what used to be
one of the wealthiest estates in Ireland, and Doe Castle are passed, and at
every half-mile most charming views are enjoyed. Lough Glen, Kilmacrenan,
Lough Salt, and Lough Fern well repay alike the lover of the beautiful and
the angler for the time and attention he can bestow upon them.

As a good illustration of the ready wit and shrewdness of the Donegal
character, we quote the following story about a ' natheral '—a term connoting
very often as much knave as fool—named Jemmy. Jemmy had been brought
up before the magistrate on a charge of poaching, only too well-founded. Once,
when carrying two fine hares in a bag, a magistrate known as 'owld Alick'
met him, and on Jemmy's assurance that the bag contained a fine fox, wished
to see him. ' Well, ye may be sure I was sore put to it, how to keep him from
catching me with the hares, and me coming aff his land ; but says I, "He's
sthrong enough, dear knows ; but he's as wicked as a tithe proctor, and if
I take him out of the bag, I wouldn't put it past him to make his
escape from both of us ; but I'll tell ye what we'll do, I'll howld the bag
for ye, and ye can put in won of yer hands and feel him ; " and I held the
mouth of the bag till him. "Will he bite ?" says he. " Troth," says I,
"ye'll have to find that out for yerself. How do I know what he *will*
do ? I'm no prophet, only I know he has nigh hand taken two of the
fingers aff *me*. But then there's a wide differ between a *poor* craythur like
me, and a magisthrate like yer honour." When owld Alick heerd tell of
biting, he wasn't so aiger for putting in his hand ; and the more he held
back the more I held forrard the mouth of the bag. At last says he,
"Jemmy, ye may take away yer fox, and here's sixpence for ye," says he,
"to drink my health in." Och, he's an amadhaun, that owld Alick, any way.'

On the other occasion Jemmy was summoned to the Dunfanaghy Petty
Sessions. 'When I came into the court house where the magisthrates were
setting, there was old Stodart, that's always hawing and humming as if he
had a bitther bad cold ; and Captain Gibbs, that's still cutting pens with a
wee knife, and letting on to mend them, so as to save the throuble of
taking notes of the thrials ; and young John Nelson, that nivir laves off
talking, only to put carrs (grimaces) on his face that would frighten an
owl ; and the clerk fella, Moran, that swears the witnesses and taches
the magisthrates what they have to do.' Jemmy's defence was that he was
not sure of a fair hearing, and hence would say nothing. This led the
magistrates into the somewhat rash promise that they would hear *whatever* he
wished to say without interrupting him. Jemmy affirms that the poaching
was done by 'a fella they call Johnny Magrory, a poaching vagabone that
lodged awhile back with Widda McCann at the cross roads, that was

married to Hudy McCann, that was son to him at the Marble Hill gate lodge, that Misther Stodart there, at the head of the honourable binch, fined for obsthructing the police. For sure Hudy angered Mr. Stodart by telling on him what was his rayson for opposing the setting up of the Government milestones along the roads—that it was to save money out of the car-drivers; for sure he knew that he couldn't bate them down in their charge for the dhriving, if they had the English milestones there to back them. And—och! yer honours, says I, don't let Misther Stodart look that way at me; for sure it wasn't me that towld of him at all, but Hudy McCann that he turned aff from keeping the gate lodge; and then she took in lodgers. And 'deed the worst lodger iver she took in was Johnny Magrory, that was no betther nor a born divil for poaching and telling lies all over the counthry. He wears a blue coat, and brass buttons on the knees of his breeches; and he towld Sally Divvor that there was no use in her going to ask Captain Gibbs for any help, for that he found it came chaper to him to swear at the people that asked for help, nor to help them; and he set his dogs on two owld weemen that came till hall dhoor to—Och! gentlemen dear, says I, don't let Captain Gibbs look that way at me, for it wasn't me that towld a word about him, but it was Johnny Magrory; and 'deed I don't belave it meself, for Captain Gibbs niver set his dogs on *me* at all, barring wonst that he was thrying to jump his horse over a rail, and he tumbled off in the shough—and that was enough to anger any one —and he wouldn't let me rub him down with my caubeen of a hat that I offered to clane him with; for, says he, "I saw ye laughing at me, ye blaggard." Ye mind, Captain? And the rid dog tore off the tail of me coat that was give me by yer honour, Misther John Nelson, when it was too rotten for ye to wear it any longer yerself. And that lying vagabone, Johnny Magrory, said ye gave it to save giving me a sixpence at an odd time, because it would be aisy for ye to say, "Have ye no conscience, Jemmy Canny, asking me again for money, and me gave ye all that good clothing a wee while ago?" And—och! yer honour, Misther Nelson, says I, don't look like that at me; for sure ye know I towld ye it wasn't me at all that said it, but that vagabone Johnny Magrory. Sure he niver tells a word of truth; and I don't know why yer honours would think that I would be setting wires and gassicks in Misther Stodart's lands, when it was Johnny Magrory done it, and not me at all.

'Well, I went on threeping (insisting) that way on the magisthrates about Johnny Magrory; and first won would get angered with me, and the others would laugh at him; and then another would get angered, and they would laugh at *him;* and when any of them would thry to stop me, I would just say, honour bright, yer honours, ye promised to hear me out. And then they couldn't help themselves, for their word was passed to hear me to the ind. And at last owld Stodart says, "We're only making a laughing-stock of ourselves, letting this fellow keep on." "But ye promised," says I; and then they all put their heads thegither, and afther awhile old Stodart says to me, "Defindant," says he, "the binch have consinted to discharge ye this time; but mind ye're niver caught poaching again, or it'll be worse for ye. Now be aff." So says I, "Sure I'll give that vagabone, Johnny Magrory, yer message, yer honours: I'll tell the poaching vagabone all ye say." And then I came away, and left them laughing at won another, and the police laughing at them all, and the people that was waiting for justice, and ivery won. They'se amadhauns, them magisthrates anyway.'[1]

After a fine ride from the Lackagh River, Mulroy Bay, in some respects the most interesting of all these fjords, is reached. Unlike Sheephaven or Lough Swilly, it is broken up by a multitude of islands, affording ever-varying and ever-fresh views. Skilful boatmen are to be had, and very enjoyable sails can be obtained on the bay. As the Atlantic is neared the shores get lower and more rocky and bare. At the extremity of the eastern headland is the little fishing village of Ballyhoorisky, inhabited by a sturdy race of fishermen, capital boatmen, ready when occasion serves to sail on the bay, to visit Tory Island, and for any other trip. One drawback is that they will chatter away in Irish to one another, and as that language sounds singularly inharmonious to a Saxon ear, the inability to understand what is said is unrelieved by sounds that in themselves are pleasing.

On one occasion the writer found himself in this out-of-the-world nook. He had come hoping for a fine day, and a long sail to Tory Island. But alas! Nature was in an unkindly mood, donning grey skies, and letting fall a drizzling rain. Beyond the village broad spurs of rock covered with heaps of sand jut out into the ocean, which was breaking upon them with considerable force. Just as we left the village a procession came down the lane. At the head walked a man in his best apparel, bearing aloft a huge wooden cross, then followed a plain coffin borne by four men; and close after this, walking two by two, all in their best dress, came what must have been nearly the whole population of the village. The funeral was plain and very touching from its absolute simplicity. It was one of those sudden unexpected incidents that give at once the charm and the value to travel, striking those deeper chords that vibrate in all hearts. Here too Death claimed his victims, here too love and sympathy and kindliness flourished. No doubt even at Ballyhoorisky the bonds of custom are strong, and some followed, possibly, on this account only; but the signs of neighbourly fellowship and interest were predominant. As the little procession wended its way over the waste, the humble cottages, the varied and subdued dresses of the mourners, the yellow sand-heaps, the bare rocks, upon which the Atlantic

---

[1] *Memoirs of a Month among the 'Mere Irish,'* pp. 290-296. This little book gives a capital notion of the life, habits, surroundings and superstitions of the Donegal natives. It is published by Kegan Paul & Co.

surges were hurling themselves in a heavy fringe of snow-white surf, stood
out in sharp contrast against the clear background of the steel-grey waters
stretched out to the distant horizon. Over all hung the dull sky, harmonizing
well with the scene of mourning, the combination uniting to form a picture
that will live long in the memory by reason of its blending together the
uncommon and beautiful in Nature with the too common manifestation of
human frailty and sorrow.

The country from Ballyhoorisky to Fanad and Port Salon on Lough
Swilly is interesting, and Lough Swilly's charms need no panegyric. In the

THE SEVEN ARCHES, LOUGH SWILLY.
From a photograph by Lawrence, of Dublin.

neighbourhood of Port Salon are the noted caverns in the cliffs which form
the Seven Arches, and a little further north is Fanad Head, confronted
on the opposite shore of the lough by Dunaff Head. From Port Salon in
the summer a steamer runs down the lough, passing Buncrana and Rathmullan to Fahan, where again the rail is touched. The scenery along the
eastern shore of the lough, and notably from Buncrana to Dunaff Head, by
way of the Gap of Mamore, is bold and attractive to the pedestrian. But
it is time we turned our steps towards Derry and Belfast, the great industrial
centres of the north of Ireland.

CHAPTER IX.

BELFAST, ARMAGH, AND LONDONDERRY.

ALTHOUGH the great and busy capital of Ulster has been left to one of the last chapters of this book, that fact must by no means be interpreted as any indication of the relative importance of that powerful centre of industry. The chief aim of the present volume has been to indicate the most picturesque parts of Ireland, giving the greater prominence to the less known and less frequented districts. But any book on the country would be imperfect which did not devote considerable space to a city second in Ireland in point of population, and in many respects the first and most important as a great centre of commercial life.

As in the case of Liverpool, Glasgow and other great ports, the growth of Belfast has been both recent and rapid. The references to it in the early records are brief and slight; in fact, its history may be said to begin about 1612, when Sir Arthur Chichester, ancestor of the present Donegal family, received from Charles I. a charter for the colony from Devonshire which he had planted on the shores of the lough. At the beginning of this century it numbered about 20,000 inhabitants, and at the last census considerably over 200,000! The day seems not far distant when it will outstrip Dublin in population.

It is admirably situated for the purposes of a great shipping centre, standing on the River Lagan, at the head of Belfast Lough. Much of the older part of the town occupies ground only a few feet above the level of the lough; and in earlier days floods were frequent, and epidemics were far too common. But improved drainage and attention to modern sanitary requirements have greatly improved this state of affairs.

Like Dublin, Belfast is rich in suburban beauty. In the eastern part of the town, and along the north shore of the lough the land slopes up from the water, reaching in the Cave Hill, which forms a very prominent object in the landscape, an elevation of over 1,100 feet. In this direction are many of the splendid houses of the rich Belfast merchants; and not

in this direction only but wherever around the city suitable sites exist, they are occupied by the men who have at once enriched themselves and built up the business prosperity of the capital of the north.

Belfast is clean and free from smoke; the streets are well laid out, and contain handsome municipal buildings, churches, colleges, shops, and private houses. The chief thoroughfares are Donegal Place, Castle Street, Donegal Street, High Street, and the most recent and finest of all, Royal Avenue.

Until the last few years Belfast was to a considerable extent open

CASTLE PLACE, BELFAST.

to the charge, that she was so engrossed in money-making and industrial enterprise as to be indifferent to her outward appearance. But if this accusation were well-grounded in the past there is little basis for it to-day. In both public and private buildings Belfast can hold her own with her great commercial rivals in the United Kingdom. Such buildings as the Custom House, the Town Hall, the new Post Office, the Belfast, the Ulster, and the Northern Banks, and the Albert Memorial are an ornament to any city. Handsome bridges also cross the Lagan.

Religion and education are zealously cared for in the city. The stranger cannot fail to be struck by the number and the excellence of the churches and colleges. Carlisle Circus is adorned with two splendid buildings; St. Enoch's Church, the finest and most imposing building belonging to the Presbyterians, and the Carlisle Memorial Church, a handsome Methodist Church, built by a wealthy merchant in commemoration of his son, who died young. On every hand Presbyterian churches are to be met with. The chief Protestant Episcopal buildings are St. George's Church in High Street, St. Ann's Church in Donegal Street, and Christ Church in College Square North. Roman Catholicism is represented by St. Malachi's in Alfred Street, and St. Patrick's in Donegal Street.

Education is represented in Belfast by the Royal Academical Institution and Government School of Art, the Queen's College, a large and commodious building, and the Model School, where over 1,200 children receive daily instruction. The special requirements of ministerial training are met by the Presbyterian College and the Methodist College. The former institution occupies a fine site at the extremity of the Botanic Avenue, and faces upon University Square. The cost was met by voluntary contributions, and it was opened by Merle d'Aubigné in 1853. The faculty consists of a president and five professors, whose chairs prior to 1871 were endowed by the State to the amount of £250 a year. Recently Magee College, at Londonderry, a large building occupying a fine site overlooking the Foyle, has been erected, and is also carried on as a college for Presbyterian ministers. A few years ago the theological professors of the two colleges were constituted 'the Presbyterian Theological Faculty (Ireland),' and 'empowered to grant the usual degrees in theology equal to those conferred by any university in the United Kingdom.'

THE ALBERT MEMORIAL.

The Methodist College, opened in 1868, cost £25,000, and is an extensive and handsome pile of buildings. It comprises a theological institute, a collegiate department in connection with Queen's College, and a boarding and day school.

It is needful that a few words should be said about the religious condition of Ireland, and these naturally occur in connection with the great Protestant stronghold of the country. The religious forces that have influenced Ireland in the past, and that are most powerfully influencing her to-day, run in the three channels represented by the Roman Catholic, the Protestant Episcopal, and the Presbyterian Churches. Of these the first is all-powerful in the south and west and in County Donegal. The second, by reason of its connection in the past with the State, has a net-work of buildings and parsonages over the whole country. The third is most powerful in Counties Antrim, Down, and Londonderry.

The Roman Catholic section far outnumbers all the others put together, comprising, according to the 1881 census, 3,951,818 adherents. It wields enormous power, owing to the fact that it forms an integral part of the life of the people, is essentially the Church of the 'Mere Irish,' and a very large proportion of the priesthood comes from the tenant farmer and peasant class.

The Protestant Episcopal Church of Ireland numbered, according to the census of 1881, 639,574 adherents. Since 1871 the supreme governing body has been the General Synod, which meets annually, and is composed of the archbishops, bishops, 208 clerical and 416 lay representatives. There are also twenty-one Diocesan Synods under the control of the General Synod. The Book of Common Prayer has been revised and slightly altered, but the Thirty-Nine Articles of the Church of England were adopted unchanged. The invested capital of the Church amounts to about £7,000,000. The great educational centre is at Trinity College, Dublin. To this Church belong many of the wealthier and of the official class of the country. The Act of 1869 severed its connection with the State, and all interested in the religious welfare of Ireland heartily wish the Episcopal Church prosperity in its reliance to a much larger extent upon voluntaryism. On the once bitterly controverted question, whether the Church should be connected with the State, and whether the disestablishment was a just act or not, opinions may, and probably do still differ. But the experience of history should give confidence for the future to all the earnest workers and well-wishers of the Episcopal Church.

The Presbyterian Church of Ireland, according to the census of 1881, numbered 485,503 adherents. Of these the vast majority reside in Central and North-eastern Ulster. Into the various Christian activities of this branch of the Church we have no space to go. Although doing good work in many parts of the country, it is chiefly among the agricultural and commercial classes of Ulster that the great body of their adherents is found. The ecclesiastical affairs are administered by the General Assembly which meets annually, having under its control thirty-six presbyteries, more than 500 churches and 600 ministers. The communicants number considerably over 100,000. It raises annually for religious and philanthropic purposes more than £150,000 a year; and it controls the two colleges already described. No careful observer can fail to see signs of still greater prosperity for this Church in the future. In addition to these three great bodies there are also scattered through the country—each body doing very good service — Methodist, Congregational, and Baptist Churches.

Belfast is not only the centre of a strong religious and philanthropic life, it is also the great

THE LINEN HALL, BELFAST.

commercial and manufacturing centre of Ireland. The linen trade is the great staple, and many large linen factories and flax-spinning mills are to be seen there. Naturally many other business occupations flourish there also. Such firms as Musgrave & Co., Marcus Ward & Co., Harland and Wolff, have a world-wide reputation. Yet, while in Belfast all the varied industries that necessarily centre in a city of over 200,000 inhabitants are to be seen in full activity, the stranger will naturally devote his attention to the two chief—the linen manufacture and ship-building. At such

A GROUP OF BELFAST OPERATIVES.

an institution as the York Street Spinning Mills he can study the former to advantage; and at Messrs. Harland and Wolff's the latter.

Belfast is a capital centre for trips to noted towns and districts in Ulster. Armagh, one of the oldest towns in Ireland, and the seat of the most ancient Irish archbishopric, is only a few miles distant. The town occupies the slopes of a hill which is very finely crowned by the handsome pile of the Cathedral. The Roman Catholic Cathedral is also magnificently placed on Banbrook Hill. The narrow streets with their ancient appearance harmonize with the great antiquity of the place. They are clean and neat, and the whole town wears an air of prosperity and extreme respectability. Dr. Reeves, a great authority on ecclesiastical affairs, writes : 'No city is so rich in historical associations, and yet has so little to show, and so little to tell in the present day, as Armagh. St. Patrick's first church is now represented by the Bank of Ireland ; the Provincial Bank comes close on St. Columba's ; St. Bride's shares its honours with a paddock ; St. Peter and St. Paul afford stabling to a modern *rus in urbe ;* and St. Mary's is lost in a dwelling-house.'

No city in Western Europe has been burnt or plundered more frequently. In very ancient days it was noted for Emania, the seat of Ulster sovereignty and of the Knights of the Red Branch, and later on for the Damhliag Mor or Great Church, built by Patrick, the great school or university, and the royal cemetery ; but except the first none of these have left any traces. The present cathedral, in all probability, stands on the site of the stone building which St. Patrick founded, and was begun about 1268. It has undergone many vicissitudes, and has been restored within comparatively recent years. It is well worth careful study, and it stands upon a site that for fourteen centuries has been consecrated to Christian worship. The Archbishop of Armagh is Primate of Ireland, and such men as Ussher, Hoadley, and Robinson have held the office.

The Giant's Causeway, the favourite trip from Belfast, will be dealt with in the next chapter. A main line of rail runs to Londonderry, passing some famous and some very pretty places. At Antrim there is a noted Round Tower, very perfect and standing in a beautiful park. Antrim Castle, near to the town, is one of the many celebrated Irish residences. It is the seat of Lord Massarene, and is situated in very lovely country. In fact, for quiet rural beauty County Antrim can take high rank. About three miles from Antrim, on the shores of Lough Neagh, stand the remains of Shane O'Neil's Castle, for ages the seat of that powerful family, and still the home of their descendants. Lough Neagh is the largest lake in the United Kingdom, being twenty miles long, twelve wide, eighty in circumference, and embracing nearly 100,000 acres. The Bann, which runs into the Atlantic through Coleraine, is the only outlet for its waters. From the picturesque point of view, the absence of mountain scenery places it at a great disadvantage when compared with many others in Ireland.

Further north still is Ballymena, a thriving town, and an important centre of the linen trade. It is the best point from which to approach classic ground in Irish story. Only three miles distant is Broughshane, inseparably linked with St. Patrick's history ; three miles further is the hill of Slemish, where Patrick lived as a slave, and where he saw those visions

and dreamed those dreams which God afterwards enabled him to put into
action for the benefit and blessing of the Irish nation.

On reaching Coleraine we have passed into the county of Derry, in
which this town holds second rank. It is prettily situated upon the Bann,
and is noted for linens, for whisky, and for salmon fishery. There is a
noted salmon leap about a mile above the town, the road to it along the
west bank forming a very pleasant walk. Much of the land in and about
the town belongs to the Irish Society. The fishery is no doubt very
profitable, but one cannot help feeling that were the salmon leap swept away
and the navigation of Lough Neagh made available by improving the

ANTRIM CASTLE.

course of the Bann, it might in the end be better for the country at
large.

The next place beyond Coleraine is Castlerock, a delightful watering
place. It possesses a beautiful sandy beach upon which the great Atlantic
rollers break in a way that affords ceaseless enjoyment to the eye and the ear.
On either hand superb views are obtained; to the east, over Port Stewart
and the Giant's Causeway; to the west, over Inishowen and the Donegal
coast around the head of Lough Foyle. It is deservedly a popular and a
favourite summer resort. There are very good drives in the neighbourhood; and traces in the way of buildings and traditions survive of the

eccentric—to put it mildly—Earl of Bristol, whom the public opinion of the last century tolerated in the See of Derry.

Derry is more closely associated with England than many other Irish towns. The Irish Society of London owns a large part of the town and neighbourhood, and has considerable influence over its affairs. The famous siege is one of the few Irish events with which every schoolboy is acquainted. The large ocean steamers of the Allan and Anchor lines call at Moville, the port of Derry. The city is also the centre of a busy industrial life. Powerful religious forces act and react upon its 30,000 inhabitants.

Derry's chief historical associations bring together a very remote and a comparatively recent past. The city is indissolubly linked to the life of

LONDONDERRY.

Columba; it did its part manfully in the seventeenth century struggle, and it exhibits to-day great activity, push and industry, strengthening rather than losing its grasp on the life of the age.

Lough Foyle is another arm of the Atlantic running inland parallel with Lough Swilly and Mulroy Bay. A few miles to the north of Londonderry it contracts into the River Foyle. A bend in the river forms upon the left bank a peninsula, and upon this hilly promontory, around which the Foyle sweeps in a fine curve, the old city was built. The hill rises to an elevation of 120 feet above the river, and makes a most picturesque site for the city. The Foyle is here a stream over 300 yards wide, and is crossed by a handsome bridge. The modern city has long since outgrown the ancient limits, has spread in all directions on the left bank, and has occupied advantageous sites on the steep slopes of the right

P

bank of the Foyle. From the hill which rises high above the bridge, on
the right bank of the Foyle, a capital bird's eye view of the city and its
surroundings may be obtained. On this bank stands the terminus of the
Coleraine and Belfast Railway. Both sides of the river are lined by quays,
for the city possesses a large coasting and colonial shipping trade. The
regular stopping of the Atlantic liners at Moville has made Derry an
emigration centre, and on the quays, as at Cork, that sight can often be
seen which is full of sinister omen for a thinly-populated country like
Ireland ; viz. groups of strong, young, able-bodied men and women, the
real stamina of the nation, waiting to embark on the tender which will ·
carry them off to the great steamer, never to return to the land of their
birth.

The name Derry is an epitome of its history. It is the anglicised
form of the Irish word *doire* or *daire*, meaning an oak-wood. It enters
into an immense number of Irish names, and wherever it occurs indicates
that once an oak forest flourished there. The pagan name was *Daire-
Calgaich*, the oak-wood of Calgach. In 546 Columba founded his
monastery here ; for centuries the old name held its ground, but about the
tenth century it was replaced by Derry-Columb-Kille. This remained the
name until the reign of James I., when the change of ownership resulted
in the change of name into *Londonderry*.[1]

As already noted, Columba was born at Gartan, a wild Donegal
district, in 521. He spent much of his boyhood at a place called Temple
Douglas, at Kilmacrenan. According to the Annals of Ulster, he founded
the church at Derry when he was only twenty-five. No trace of the
original building, which was known as the Black Church, survives. 'Its
Round Tower was standing in the seventeenth century, but the only record
of its existence now remaining is the name of the lane which leads to its
site, the Long Steeple.'[2]

Londonderry practically dates from the Plantation of Ulster. The
county was held in early times by the O'Cathans, or O'Kanes, who were
tributary to the O'Neils. Upon the overthrow of that powerful sept, and
the confiscation of their estates in 1609, Derry, Coleraine, and the adjacent
territory were awarded to the citizens of London, sixty out of every
thousand acres being reserved for the Church, and some portions being
given to three native Irish gentlemen. The Common Council of London
agreed to spend £20,000 upon the district, appointed twenty-six men to
manage it, and called them the Irish Society, kept for itself Derry and
Coleraine, and parted the rest of the land amongst twelve of the London
Livery Companies. In 1637 their charter was cancelled ; Cromwell
restored the Society, and Charles II. granted a new charter. Over
150,000 acres are thus held by the Irish Society and the Companies, among

[1] See *Irish Names of Places* (Joyce), pp. 503, 504.   [2] Reeves' edition of Adamnan's *Life of Columba*, p. 277.

the latter the chief proprietors being the Skinners, 34,000, the Drapers 27,000, the Mercers 21,000, and the Fishmongers 20,000.

London soon began those works which have fastened its name upon Derry. In 1609 the walls were built at a cost of over £8,000. They are still perfect, and now form a pleasant promenade about a mile in extent. There are six gates. These walls are associated with the famous siege, and upon them stand the lofty monument to the Rev. George Walker and the old gun known as Roaring Meg. Into the story of the siege of 1689, which lasted 105 days, of the sufferings endured by the garrison, of their heroism, and of the final battle at the Vorn which raised the siege, we have no space to enter in detail. For popular purposes Macaulay's account is perhaps sufficient; those who wish to make a special study of it cannot do better than consult Dr. Witherow's *Derry and Enniskillen in 1689.*

THE BISHOP'S GATE, LONDONDERRY.

The Cathedral of Derry owes its existence to London. It dates from 1633, and in the porch, which also contains a bombshell fired into the town during the siege, stands a tablet which runs :

BOMBSHELL AND TABLET IN THE PORCH OF LONDONDERRY CATHEDRAL.

If stones could speak, then London's praise
  should sound,
Who built this church and city from the
  ground.

The building consists of a nave and two aisles separated from each other by pointed arches. It has been recently enlarged by the addition of a choir. Over the entrance is a large organ with very finely-carved wood, said to have been taken from one of the Armada wrecks. A large tower surmounted by a spire stands at the western end of the cathedral. From the top of the tower a splendid view is obtained. The whole city lies at the observer's feet, enabling him to recognise readily all the important buildings and sites, and to watch the various signs of commercial activity. At the same time he commands on every side a wide prospect over the pretty surrounding country.

A very extensive shirt manufacture is carried on in Derry, not the weaving process, but the making up of all

kinds of shirts. The factories are very large, and employ a considerable number of hands, a very large proportion being women

ROARING MEG AND WALKER'S MONUMENT, LONDONDERRY.

and girls. A visit to one of them introduces the stranger to many processes of interest. The ingenious knives for cutting out large quantities of collars, cuffs, &c., at a time, the minute subdivision of labour, the enormous number of sewing machines, and its general air of rapid work and prosperous trade have a stimulating effect, after a journey through the wilds of Donegal or Connemara.

CARRICK A REDE.

CHAPTER X.

THE GIANT'S CAUSEWAY AND THE MOURNE MOUNTAINS.

THE Giant's Causeway is the only part of Ireland which rivals Killarney in wide-spread fame and in general popularity. The traveller who has reached Belfast by the rapid and comfortable express train on the Great Northern Railway, or who has come from Fleetwood direct by boat, has two routes open to him; direct by rail, or along what is called the Coast Drive. Should he come by the shortest sea-route, viz., from Stranraer to Larne, at the latter place he is already one stage on the journey. If time presses, the quickest route is by the Belfast and Northern Counties Railway to Portrush. But if the weather be fine and time no great object, by far the best, and for the lover of the beautiful the most enjoyable route is to follow the Coast Road from Larne to the Causeway.

Portrush, only a few miles north of Coleraine, is a fashionable and popular sea-side resort. It is connected with the Causeway by an electric tramway, the first built in the United Kingdom. This is worked from Bushmills, and has been planned so as to enable visitors to enjoy as much as possible of the fine coast scenery which is passed during the ride. The line begins to ascend very soon after leaving Portrush, and splendid views over the coast and the ocean are obtained. At a distance of three and a half miles, the first 'lion' of the district appears, Dunluce Castle, the ancient stronghold of the M'Quillans. It is an extremely picturesque ruin, standing upon the very verge of a cliff which rises high above the sea, and which is connected with the mainland only by an arch forming a path about eighteen inches wide. The cluster of gables, walls, arches and towers, all in a decidedly ruinous condition, is most effective; and it is well to be content with the distant view. Closer inspection adds nothing to the charm as a compensation for the nervous excitement of crossing the narrow arch.

Two or three miles further the line strikes inland, and Bushmills, the headquarters of the tramway company, is reached. All who are interested in the practical working of the line should stop here long enough to inspect the building where the electricity is generated. That it is generated may be proved, not only by the demonstration of being carried there in a car supplied with no other motive force, but by taking slight shocks from the rail.

Bushmills is a neat little place, noted, like Coleraine, for distilling, and also for salmon fishing. The River Bush runs past it into the ocean, and about a mile above the town rushes impetuously on its way through a beautiful little glen, thus forming a salmon leap. The old mills stood here, but they were removed to make room for the apparatus by which the electricity is generated. The water from the upper reaches of the river is brought to the building by a race, and a head of twenty-six feet of water is obtained. By this means driving force which can be worked up to a hundred horse-power is obtained, and by an ingenious mechanical arrangement it is imparted to the powerful dynamos in the building. The supply can be easily regulated, and the testing instruments are all very interesting. The very pretty surroundings enhance the pleasure of a visit.

From Bushmills a short run takes the car to the terminus, which is only a stone's throw from the Causeway Hotel. Since the opening of the tramway, this has been greatly improved. The writer recalls a visit some years ago, when after a long day's drive, the latter part through mist and rain, he arrived damp and weary, and found the appearance of hotel and rooms extremely depressing, and the lack of creature comforts very considerable. He recently spent a night there, and although it rained a deluge and blew a hurricane, the snugness was all that could be desired. The whole place has been refurnished, new reception rooms added, and the cheerful electric light, supplied from Bushmills, now adds greatly to the comfort of the visitor.

The Causeway, like Killarney, suffers from a plague of guides. Escape from them is well-nigh impossible. The best thing is to take one from the hotel, and keep rigidly to the arrangement by which his services are included in the bill. It is a great misfortune that the visitor should not be able to roam at will about this magnificent piece of coast scenery. There are few places better fitted to arouse wonder at the marvellous works of God in Nature ; there are few spots even along the grand west coast that contain so much to delight the eye and the mind. But the horde of guides, and the constant expectation that the next turn of the path will bring you either to a beggar, or a seller of spring water, or to a vendor of the minerals of the neighbourhood, goes far to banish all the higher enjoyments of the place.

The first view of the Causeway is not unfrequently such a contrast to what imagination has pictured, that there is disappointment and a temptation to run to extremes in denouncing previous descriptions. But as the true nature of the coast is comprehended, as the beautiful forms of the pillars are appreciated, and as one after another the many geological marvels of the region are noted, these feelings disappear. In their place comes a truer realisation of the grandeur of the scene. 'Along the north coast,' writes Professor Hull, 'the scenery is often bold and striking ; sometimes, as in the neighbourhood of the Giant's Causeway, the cliffs rise from the sea in a series of terraces of dark columnar basalt, with vertical walls, and separated from each other by bands of reddish bole, or volcanic ash. These great beds or terraces represent successive lava flows, and they differ from one another not only in thickness but in the size and arrangement of the columns. At other times, as at Fair Head, directly opposite the Mull of Kintyre, huge columns of basalt descend from the top of the cliff in one or two sheer vertical sweeps for several hundred feet, while at the base of the cliff the shore is strewn with broken columns of trap heaped up in wild confusion : a Titanic breakwater which the waves of the sea have reared up against their own advance.'[1]

The best way to get a good general idea of the beauty and boldness of the coast about the Causeway is to take a boat and row westwards to Porthcoon and to Dunkerry Caves. The boat can easily enter both in fine

[1] *Physical Geography of Ireland*, pp. 61, 62.

weather, the only time when the row is practicable. Porthcoon is 350 feet long and 45 high, and exhibits fine colouring, owing to the presence in the rocks of peroxide of iron. Dunkerry is much larger, being 600 feet long and 96 feet high. To those who like this class of natural phenomena the trip may be recommended ; others may be apt to feel that there is in the caves hardly enough to compensate for the boat trip, the damp atmosphere, the rather strong sea-weedy odours, and the persistent way in which the boatmen try to sell you boxes of geological specimens, which are utterly unreliable, and probably have been carried to the Causeway with an eye to large profits.

On leaving the caves, the boat turns eastwards and runs along the splendid coast for either a short or a long trip, as the traveller decides. Those who enjoy being on the water should extend the trip as far as Benmore or Fair Head. The usual excursion is much shorter. Running past the Causeway proper all the bays and headlands as far as Pleaskin are seen, and then the boat returns and lands the passengers upon the Causeway. This consists of an enormous number—about 40,000—of basaltic columns, only a few feet above the level of the sea, jutting out from the cliffs of the same formation, rising two or three hundred feet immediately behind them. They gradually sink beneath the waves, forming a most magnificent natural pier. How far beneath the waves they extend is not known. But as the same formation exists at Staffa, it is commonly supposed that they extend across to the Scotch coast. The Celtic imagination has settled that the Causeway was the work of the giant Fin McCoul, whose Scotch rival boasted of his ability to thrash him, but objected to getting wet in crossing over to do so. Whereupon Fin magnanimously built the Causeway and defeated his rival. In later days, on the disappearance of the giants, the Causeway sank beneath the waves.

A perverse ingenuity is shown here in twisting every group of pillars into some connection with the giant. Just as at Killarney one is pestered with the O'Donoghue's honeycomb and book and pulpit, &c., so is it here *ad nauseam.* The giant's loom, and gateway, and organ, &c. &c., are indicated by the loquacious guide, who generally accompanies his absurd information with the query as to whether his victim has ever seen anything so fine before in his life. If the proprietors of the Causeway Hotel could provide a few intelligent men, able to point out the geological marvels of the district with some approach to accuracy, they would confer a boon upon travellers. Large numbers who visit the Causeway despise the nonsense that is talked at present ; but for want of knowing exactly what to see, they fail altogether to appreciate the unique claims which the Causeway has upon our wonder and admiration.

It ought, in fairness to the guides, to be mentioned that when upon the Causeway itself they do enable the visitor who displays any interest in the subject to appreciate the wonderful regularity of formation of the pillars, and the beautiful way in which they are grouped. The ladies' chair, the fan, the honeycomb, &c., are their fanciful names for what are very striking arrangements of the pillars. The guides also assert that there is only *one* triangular pillar, *three* with nine sides, comparatively few with four and eight sides, the overwhelming majority having either five, six, or seven sides.

THE LADIES' CHAIR, GIANT'S CAUSEWAY.

The clusters known as the Giant's Loom and Gateway stand at the eastern cliff end of the Causeway, and are beautiful specimens of the formation. A splendid cluster on the face of the cliff is called the Giant's Organ. In one part, instead of the vertical, a horizontal formation can be clearly seen, the ends of the pillars being at right angles to the cliff.

But fully as wonderful as the Causeway, and much more impressive, are the mighty masses of the Amphitheatre, a superb semicircular cliff, in which the pillars occur in stages ; the Chimneys, a cluster of pillars standing on the apex of a bold headland ; and the grand cliff, nearly 400 feet high, named Pleaskin Head. All along these cliffs the pillar clusters and masses of richly-coloured rocks, seen under a bright sky, and washed by a sunlit sea, constitute a gallery of the most delightful and exhilarating natural pictures.

But we must push on, and follow the road along the coast to Larne. Just

THE HORIZONTAL FORMATION, GIANT'S CAUSEWAY.

as in Nor-
way, tra-
vellers,
wishing to
see the
Romsdal to
perfection
should ap-
proach it
through the
quieter
scenery of
the Gud-
brandsdal,
so the Causeway
should be ap-
proached rather than
left by this route.
It is true that Fair
Head is grander far
than anything the

PLEASKIN HEAD, GIANT'S CAUSEWAY.

Causeway can show,
but that is really a
part of the same piece
of coast. The road
passes many points of
interest which can
only be inspected by
the leisurely wayfarer.
Dunseverick Castle,
and Carrick a Rede,
the island which can
only be reached by
the perilous swinging
bridge, are within easy
reach of the Cause-
way. For Fair Head
Ballycastle is the
starting-point, a little
town where good ac-
commodation is to be
had. It is also a good
point from which to
reach Rathlin Island,
another of those coast
trips which depend so

GREY MAN'S PATH.

entirely upon the weather. The island possesses very fine cliffs, and only one harbour, which is unavailable during westerly winds, the commonest along this coast. Columba, here as in so many other places, is said to have founded a church; and Robert Bruce not only found a safe refuge on the island, but is also said to have derived his encouragement from the famous persevering spider while concealed in the castle still known by his name.

Benmore, or Fair Head, is fitly described as the climax of the Antrim coast. It rises 639 feet above the sea, and half of this is taken up by huge columns of greenstone 30 feet wide. Through an enormous chasm in the cliff a path runs, by which a good view of the face of the headland is obtained. It may be explored without danger, if reasonable care is exercised. Across the top of the chasm, which is called the Grey Man's Path, a huge pillar has fallen, forming a natural bridge. From the top of the headland is a magnificent view extending to the Scotch coast, and over Rathlin Island, and away beyond the Causeway to the distant shores of Inishowen.

Leaving Ballycastle, the road runs through pleasant country by way of Cushendun and Cushendall to the coast, which it then skirts closely all the way to Larne. It first passes around Red Bay and Garron Point. Here is Garron Tower, built by the late Frances Ann, Marchioness of Londonderry, and bequeathed by her to a younger brother of the present marquis. From Garron Point to Glenarm a constant succession of very charming views are enjoyed, the sea and coast scenery being every here and there varied by beautiful inland peeps.

Larne is well-situated, and has a good harbour. Hence the return journey to Belfast is made by way of Carrickfergus and White Abbey. At the former there are some very interesting remains, the chief being the old Anglo-Norman castle; it dates from 1178, and occupies a strong position on a rock which overlooks Belfast Lough.

One other beautiful district of Ireland lies within easy reach of Belfast, viz., Rostrevor and the Mourne Mountains. This district lies between Belfast and Carlingford Loughs. The latter is very beautiful, the shores being well-wooded, and the hills rising steeply from the water. The town of Carlingford lies on the southern shore, and, like Carrickfergus, contains an ancient Anglo-Norman castle, but not in such a good state of preservation. On the north shore is Rostrevor, a noted and very lovely little watering place. There are not wanting those who put it at the head of the watering places of the United Kingdom. The little town stands between two rivers, and behind it Rostrevor Mountain rises up nearly 1,600 feet. The railroad ends at Warrenpoint, four miles from Rostrevor, and a splendid drive can be taken around the coast to Newcastle, where the railroad from Downpatrick stops. By this route Kilkeel is passed. Newcastle is a formidable rival to Rostrevor, and is the best point from whence to visit Slieve Donard, the highest point of the Mourne Mountains. It attains a height of 2,796 feet, and affords a view of great extent, not only over the whole group of mountains of which it forms a part, but inland, over Newry to Slieve Gullion; to the north over the fertile County Down; to the south as far as Howth; and over the Irish Sea to the hills of the Isle of Man. On the return journey to Belfast, Downpatrick should by all means be visited. Here, according to the *Tripartite Life*, St. Patrick was buried, and tradition, with less probability, asserts that St. Columba and St. Brigid were also interred here. St. Patrick founded a monastery at Downpatrick very early in his Irish labours. The present cathedral dates only from 1790. A very fine rath exists in the town, and a Druidic Ring, only three miles distant. On the road to this are the Wells of Struel, a famous place of pilgrimage.

'FAREWELL, YER HONOUR!'
From a Sketch by Charles Whymper.

INDEX.

LONDON: WILLIAM CLOWES AND SONS, LIMITED, STAMFORD STREET AND CHARING CROSS.

www.ingramcontent.com/pod-product-compliance
Lightning Source LLC
Chambersburg PA
CBHW030124030726

47498CB00007B/2537